to
Sylvia, - Xmas

I hope this will be useful to
a seasoned angler.
Love Jean

THE WOMAN'S GUIDE TO ANGLING

THE WOMAN'S GUIDE TO ANGLING

Judith Milner

Illustrations by Dave Rudd

Thomas Harmsworth Publishing Company,
Stoke Abbott

British Library Cataloguing in Publication Data
Milner, Judith
    The Woman's Guide to Angling
    I. Title II. Rudd, Dave
    799.1082

    ISBN 0-948807-17-2

Printed and bound in Great Britain by
Bookcraft (Bath) Ltd.

I would like to dedicate this book to Brian, my husband, who has given me as much support while I was writing it as he has always given me with my fishing.

Acknowledgements

We are grateful for permission to reproduce brief extracts from
the following books:

Days on Sea, Loch and River by Muriel Foster, Michael Joseph
The Penguin Guide to Fishing by Colin Willcock, Penguin
Books
Fly Fishers' Life by Charles Ritz, The Bodley Head
Sea Trout Fishing by Hugh Falkus, H.F. & G. Witherby Ltd.
Fishing in Eden by W. Nelson, H.F. & G. Witherby Ltd.
Catching Salmon by Richard Waddington, David & Charles
Publishers
Plank Bridge by the Pool by N. Thelwell, Methuen London
The Treasury of Angling by L. Koller, Hamlyn Publishing, part
of Reed International Books

CONTENTS

PREFACE

I have been fishing for some forty years and during that time have read many books on the subject. Most books on fishing tend to be a bit technical in their content, and unless you are a hardened fisher reader, I can imagine most books being returned to the bookshelf or to the library whence they came, after the reader has completed the first chapter. Good books on the sport of angling are hard to come by: one wants to read something and at the end of it can't wait to get to the waterside to make the first catch.

The Woman's Guide to Angling has so much content, all of which is required by the beginner. It covers many subjects, from pollution in rivers to stocking of rivers, how to catch your fish, where to catch your fish - and it is impossible for me to comment on all of it. It is written with wit and charm, and this does not surprise me, having been acquainted with Judith and her husband for some twenty years. Judith and I have had many discussions on fishing and related matters, and having read the manuscript that you are about to read we are no doubt going to have more. In particular, I must discuss grayling fishing with her and perhaps I can change her mind about the poor creature.

Fishing is sport to be enjoyed and to do that you must have a sense of humour. In my job as a ghillie I have fished with numerous ladies over the years and, with the exception of the odd one, most have seen the funny side of fishing. One story which comes to mind is of a lady who was being taught to spin salmon in the early spring. At that time of the year the bait

PREFACE

must be fished very slow and deep, so my colleague by whom she was being taught persistently told her 'you're winding too hard, you're winding too hard.' After half an hour of this, at the end of a cast, the lady wound the bait in, swung round in the boat, dangling the bait in front of his nose, and said wryly, 'Is that slow enough now?' Lo and behold, on the end of the hook was a water snail!

Having said all this, fishing is a serious sport and people do it for various reasons. After reading this book, you may decide to join the fishing fraternity and if you do you will be joining a large group of dedicated people who have done more for conservation than any other body or government.

Tight Lines!

Kenneth Jack
Roxburghshire

CHAPTER ONE

INTRODUCTION

What is fishing anyway?
Richard Gordon once commented that there are two types of
book on fishing - science fiction and romantic fiction. He is
only 95% correct in my opinion. Certainly a distinction can
be made between anglers and people who are just fishermen,
who are only interested in how many fish they catch, use the
latest gadgetry and aim for the most and biggest fish. They are
beneath the contempt of most anglers - who are a different
breed altogether but not entirely to be dismissed as hopeless
romantics.

I think there is a philosophical side to angling but it is hard
to convey this on paper without sounding incurably soppy and
romantic. David Profumo comes closer than most in his
Telegraph articles. Although he ends one account of a memo-
rable fish with the words, 'Reader, I landed it,' displaying
distinct romantic tendencies, he does try to explain why
catching fish is only partly concerned with angling.

As a sport it dates from 2000 BC but only in England has
it been elevated to a passionate art form and become intensely
associated with writing. He thinks that angling re-enacts the
childhood dream of chasing the invisible. It involves the angler
in an alien world from which all life evolved, and in its
extraordinary combination of hope and impotence it offers the
human imagination a ritual to express the 'dance macabre'
that attends everyday life. To the non-addict, this probably
sounds like claptrap but I believe every word because that is

1

what it feels like to me.

And not only me. This philosophical theme is echoed down the years in many angling books. The first person to put pen to paper on the subject in this country was, of course, a woman. Dame Juliana Berners commented in the fifteenth century:

'Thus have I pouvyd in myn entent that the dyspote and game of anglyne is the very meane and cause that enducith a man in to a mery spyryte.'

Anglers, being mostly men, prefer to consider Isaak Walton as the guru of angling and, in fairness to him, he does have some pretty sensible things to say about angling. He not only thinks that it is a rest to the mind, a cheerer of spirits, a diverter of sadness, a calmer of unquiet thoughts, a moderator of passions, a procurer of contentedness and a recipe for patience and peace but he also expresses some sentiments which might not find much favour in our current political and social clime:

'There are many now that by others taken to be serious grave men, which we contemn and pitie; men of sowre complexions; money-getting-men, that spend all their time first in getting, and next in anxious care to keep it: men that are condemn'd to be rich, and always discontented, or busie. For these poor-rich-men, wee Anglers pitie them.'

I couldn't agree with him more. Angling does restore the soul and it is not romantic to think like this. Also, can you name another male activity which enables men to express their feelings more openly? For the true angler, there is no machismo, no need to prove oneself against others, no need to rush about. Angling is not necessarily tranquil but does aid tranquillity of mind. It certainly highlights a person's character too as it is impossible to be an angler (as opposed to a fisher) if honesty, charity and a well worked out philosophy of life are not present.

Your behaviour is so exposed in angling and you have to face up to your character faults very quickly. In my first full year of angling I met with mostly gentle, helpful people. Sometimes too helpful. One day I was casting inexpertly down stream whilst an elderly gentleman some sixty yards away was casting a superb line upstream. A fish rose equidistant between us at which point he doffed his cap and called 'your fish I think,' promptly reeling in his line and moving elsewhere. My chances of casting over the fish were non-existent but I learnt how to respect space that day.

The following week, I was tackling up with my husband when we were approached by a club member and the usual discussion about our chances began. We told him that my husband had a very good fish on the main pool the day before and then set off leisurely to the river. On our way, we decided not to fish the same pool as it would be only fair to let the newcomer have first go. Our charitable intentions were in vain as we saw him running along the top of the field to get to the pool before us! A fisherman, of course. We pitied him.

You can't cheat in angling because the only person you would cheat is yourself. And you must practise charity because it is not acceptable to go home with more fish than you can eat. A bumper day means that you can stop fishing, put fish back carefully or give them away to friends. This latter can be a useful exercise in pride and humility as an extremely skilled angler friend of ours found out. He was in the habit of giving his catch to the farmer who let him drive his car close to the river and tried to take enough to feed the large family. One day he caught only one fish but one to be really proud of, a much larger than average trout for that particular river, a veritable monster - well worth boasting about. He laid his prize on the farmer's table proudly at the end of the day, gazing with awe at the wonderful creature. He was swiftly brought down to earth by the farmer's comment 'What, only one today? Losing your touch a bit aren't you?'

And angling is also good exercise. It is like yoga with exciting bursts - quite aerobic. You have to be calm to concentrate on the line, it is absolutely no good standing there muttering 'bite, you bugger, bite,' because it won't. You have to achieve calmness but the beauty is that this leads to intense excitement and then calmness again. It must be good for the heart as well as the mind. In fact, angling is a combination of contemplation and action and I can't think why I am telling you about it. I should keep such a good thing to myself. Perhaps it is my generous angler's charity - an unworthy thought, it is the simple end product of angling addiction. As is obvious, the link between angling and writing is strong in this country to the point of compulsion. A need to share the dream.

Is it cruel?

This sort of lyrical enthusiasm for angling must seem pretty stupid and hypocritical to anyone who is interested in the conservation of wild life. Even if you aren't into saving elephants and seals, the question still remains about whether or not angling is a blood sport and what sort of justification can be made for killing living creatures - even if all the philosophical points about it being good for humans are accepted.

A not unusual reaction to hearing that I am an angler is, 'I tried it once but I couldn't bring myself to kill the poor thing.' There is a mixture of squeamishness and distaste for killing a living creature, even from the everyday person who happily eats meat. There are all sorts of sophisticated rationalisations for angling and killing fish. Some naturalists such as Thelwell, who has created his own lake and almost given up angling on finding how pleasurable it is to watch a pond unfold and come to life, argues that life itself is inherently cruel.

Whilst he admits that the whole question of killing is complex and disturbing he says that life for all creatures in the water is precarious in the extreme, an endless sequence of kill or be killed. He manages to reconcile the sobering thought of removing a bright existence for ever by holding a responsible attitude towards replacing fresh stock. He says:

'. . . for the more one comes to admire and respect the fish and to feel an obligation to preserve them for future generations to enjoy.'

4

He is quite correct in that anglers are indubitably the most effective fish conservationists in the whole world. Without the angling lobby, trout and salmon would have vanished under the depredations of commercial fishing long ago. But, even so, this is a spurious justification, really no more than a simple ends justifying means argument which we all know to be open to endless manipulation to carry on doing harmful things.

And the idea of respecting the fish is a bit dubious too. It's rather Ernest Hemingway, elevating the prey into a noble creature against which man has to pit his wits and may the most noble animal win. After an enormous tussle with a fish, one does get a tendency to get a bit carried away with the nature of the fight itself and this leads one to personalise the fish a little and imagine that it performed human behaviours, such as sulking. And a newly landed fish can be a beautiful thing. I can't help but admire some of the fresh, sparkling fish which I have caught.

Still, I can't honestly say that it has been a noble struggle between equal partners. Usually the fish has the advantage anyway - not that that justifies my going after it - I could always leave it alone and let 'nature' sort out which fish lives and which fish dies. My intervention and any conservation effects are to do with my selfish desire to keep fish around so that I can continue to have a go at catching them. This is not quite the same as actually catching them, but that's a bit of angling complexity which is hard for the non-addict to grasp.

Whilst the sight of salmon jumping in a pool is indeed an awe-inspiring sight, it would be wrong to imbue fish with nobility. They are cold blooded creatures in every sense of the word. They spend most of their time lying in the easiest bit of water, eating as many of their fellow creatures that they can manage with the least possible expenditure of energy. As Nelson (1922) comments:

'Fish do not stand high in comparison with other animals in intelligence. Life under water is not conducive to the growth of great intelligence. The environment of fresh water fish is very restricted. Except in regard to competition for food there is little of a stimulative character in their lives. The great and enlivening sense of hearing is absent. The sight of the fish is set in a fixed stare. It does not change its direction or dimension, and it is unaccommodating in regard to the judgement of distance. The overpowering motive of life is feeding.'

And this mode of life does not ennoble them either. The most successful fish, those which have lived the longest and eaten the most of their own kind, are ugly creatures with dark flanks, hooked jaws and saggy bellies. It would be rather fitting if the most successful anglers turned out somewhat similar.

No, I can't pretend to share any of these rationalisations at all. Still, I do think that angling is not really a blood sport like others. Mainly I suppose because I agree with Juliana Berners that it is a superior activity to the average blood sport. She compares angling favourably with hunting, falconry and fowling but her main argument is about the way in which the activity is conducted. She obviously thinks other blood sports

. . . ugly creatures with dark flanks, hooked jaws and saggy bellies . . .

are quite barbaric, unseemly and harmful to the nature. On hunting she says:

'For the hunter must alwaye renne and folowe his houndes, traueyllynge and swettynge full sore. He blowyth tyle his lyppes blyster. And whan he wenyth it be an hare full oft it is a hegge hogge. Thus he chasyth and wote not what. He comyth home at euyn rayn beten pryckyd: and his clothes torn wete shode all myry. Some hounds loste: some surbat.'

I may not be fully convinced that angling is not a blood sport but I certainly cannot see that it has anything in common with other blood sports. And it's not as though we anglers necessarily catch much. Juliana Berners says that there are twelve impediments to fishing: poor equipment; poor baits; fishing at non-biting time; letting the fish see you; thick, flood water; fish not moving in the cold; hot weather; rain; hail or deep snow; tempest; great wind; and an east wind. And my friend, Barbara Brearley, would add that I can come up with many more excuses for my failure to catch fish.

As I said earlier, there is more to angling than catching fish. Yet the cruelty aspect remains. The fish don't actually feel very much from the hook which is in a bony part of the mouth. In fact, when my friend, Lewis Ann Garner, hooked herself deeply in the temple she said that it did not hurt in the least despite my clumsy efforts to heave the hook out. There is no way that fish would leap about so energetically if it hurt. But I don't suppose that they like it particularly either. Paul Gibson, now a ghillie on the Dee, always refuses to net a fish until it totally surrenders. He points out that the fish is fighting for its life and likes to see a certain amount of fairness about the whole matter. Also, most anglers don't get upset if the fish gets off the hook. The angler might curse him or herself but the fish is wished well.

I accept that it is cruel to some extent and I suppose my justification, in so far as I have one, is that I eat the fish I catch. Most people who think it cruel don't hesitate to eat dead fish from supermarkets or order trout in restaurants. If you do this, then you can't argue about me. At least I am nearer to the reality of eating flesh than you are with your cling film wrapped, supermarket fish with its head off and guts removed.

What I really can't understand is people who put fish back. Again a little bit of double standards because I return small fish and kelts (salmon which have spawned and are returning to the sea). A whole trip to America was ruined because of a modern policy of returning fish to preserve stocks. I couldn't see why we were permitted to fish at all if fish stocks were so threatened.

Similarly, I do not understand coarse anglers. These are people who catch fish which are not edible, keep them in nets, weigh the catch and then return them to the water. One carp was declared the best fish caught in Ireland two years running! It seems an odd sort of life for a fish to be specimen hunted annually by 'anglers.' I am assured that the fish don't suffer but I still can't see the point in it although I know that I must be careful as there is a class element in this - coarse fishing is cheaper than game angling and there are male tensions between the two groups. Richard Walker, the doyen of coarse fishers, writing about salmon, comments that he does not care for the company they keep:

'If a man enjoys salmon fishing and can afford it, good luck to him, but when he starts putting on airs and throwing his weight about because of it, I prefer his room to his company. Most rod caught salmon are taken by men whose money compensates for their ignorance, (rather) than by skilful anglers.'

Ouch! I had always thought that it was rather nice that any beginner can catch a salmon. That the salmon makes the decision whether or not to catch you and usually is in full control of the subsequent battle did, I thought, marginally reduce the blood sport argument. Still, Richard Walker's book is called *No Need to Lie* and is about specimen fish he caught. I can't see what anglers would have to lie about anyway - you either believe yourself or you don't. I suppose that coarse fish must have been eaten at some time because monks kept carp ponds. And Mrs Gaskell has her heroine's mother averting domestic disaster and breathing again in *North and South* because of carp:

'The clouds on her mother's brow had cleared off under the propitious influence of a brace of carp, most opportunely presented by a neighbour.'

Yet, Francis Francis commented in the nineteenth century that carp is not worth eating, being 'a muddy, bony, wooly beast on whom sauce or condiment is simply wasted.' And even Isaak Walton only accepted pike when it has been cooked with herbs, pickled oysters, anchovies, butter and oranges. I did have a sneaking suspicion that the monks kept the carp for the poor people and ate something better themselves but can't bring myself to doubt Mrs Gaskell. All I can conclude is that it was nothing short of a miracle that Margaret still got a proposal of marriage after her suitor was given carp for luncheon.

Also, coarse fish tend to live in slow moving, muddy water, semi-stagnant ponds or canals and the baits used are maggots, cheese, bread paste and luncheon meat. These fish are caught during the winter and the fisher is fairly passive, sitting for ages on the bank, often into the dead of night, waiting for the fish to bite. I wouldn't go quite as far as Joan Clarkson's 'benevolent uncle' in *Back Casts and Back Chat,* whom she assures us held strong feelings about coarse fishing:

' "Coarse fishing," resumed the Benevolent Uncle, reaching for the yellow silk, "was invented to evade the laws against sleeping out. As mendicancy is tolerated if accompanied by song, so sleeping out is respectable if done in the presence of rod and line." '

But to me, coarse fishing does not add up to angling and the negative helps me define quite what angling is for me. Game fish inhabit the purest, most sparkling water - something we are all aware that is in short supply at the moment - and it is this desire to reach out to the clean source of rivers and their life that particularly appeals to game anglers.

It is cruel to some extent, whatever my rationalisations, but the fish is the point at which I connect with the life of the water. Looking at the wild life or swimming in the water would not enable me to make that connection - that thin, fine line which links me with life below the water surface. There is nothing else in life quite like it and I can assure you that it has nothing in common with hunting and shooting. In the final analysis, it is about as irrational as boxing - people disapprove of boxing but still engage in it or watch boxing matches.

If you are still unconvinced about this, give me a ring and I will give you a fresh fish. This has marked effects on my critical colleagues. One who was extolling the virtues of vegetarianism happily took two trout home to eat on the grounds that they were not battery reared. And that's another ball game. Modern meat production is indubitably cruel but fish is cheap and the only sort of meat many people can afford. Most principles are costly and complex.

Why women?
Most people seem to find it faintly ludicrous that I am an angler. The usual comment is 'do you fish too?' to which I now reply 'if its good enough for the Queen Mother . . .' whilst my husband turns it on its head and says 'no, but I fish too.' The notion that angling is something men do is firmly fixed. Even Juliana Berners' book was only attributed to her because it was considered, on an ungallant hypothesis, that only a woman could have given such directions for making a rod and that no man could have been guilty of so many *non sequiturs* in many of the book's arguments!

Actually, women have always been anglers and their current ranks include Fiona Armstrong, Viscountess Astor, and Diana Rigg. Women are more prominent in salmon angling than in other branches and they hold all the records. The biggest salmon ever caught in the UK was caught by Miss Georgina Ballantine on the Tay.

INTRODUCTION

I am ashamed to report that a woman actually entered a coarse fishing competition (anglers don't really compete with anyone other than themselves) but she was persuaded by her husband who lent her a rod and bait. Thus, Mrs B W (delicacy forbids me to name her) broke the British catch record in 1975 with 304 fish in three and a half hours. She also landed the biggest roach of the day. And, in 1993, a seven year old girl landed three carp (all over 10 lbs) in a single day.

I much prefer the story printed in the letters section of *Salmon, Trout and Sea Trout* following a lively article on women's superior angling skills:

'A lady of my acquaintance joined a party of gentlemen fishing the river Vosso in Norway. At the end of her stay she had killed 13 out of the 17 salmon taken. During the week, seeing the way things were going, the men banished her to Lake Evanger, which flows into the Vosso and in which, I understand, few fish are caught. The day was hot and windless, so she contented herself with sunbathing in the boat (which the ghillie rowed round the lake) trailing a large lure behind with the line tied round her big toe. Using this interesting and novel technique, she hooked and landed a 36lb salmon. What more can one say?'

Anthony J Duncan, Banchory

Indeed, what more can one say? This sort of story is not uncommon but many male anglers still seem to entertain doubts. In *Trout and Salmon,* Logie Bruce Lockhart, even in July 1988, is guilty of the most appalling sexism. He writes:

'I always thought my pupil Linda would be a success. She was, and still is, the kind of bright, slender blonde who turns every sixth former's head. It seemed she would make a splash on television or the stage; I wouldn't have guessed she would excel at anything as serious as salmon fishing.'

The fact of the matter is that women not only catch the biggest, and the most fish, but they do not fish as aggressively as men. Wilma Paterson and Peter Behan (1990) put it down

11

to pheromones but I am more in favour of simpler explanations. Such as: men are only surprised that women fish at all because few of them take it up until later on in life. I started as a child when my brothers did but was soon discouraged by their scathing comments and their traditional attitude towards girls - you can join in if you don't mind being the indian, the boundary fielder, the helpmate etc. Also, girls are rarely allowed to wander off along a river bank on their own. Then children come along and there is nothing more antipathetic to angling than the presence of children. So, you tend to take it up in middle life, usually along with your husband.

John Ashley Cooper, the most famous of modern anglers, has a simple explanation for women's success in angling. He argues that there are three main qualifications in angling which lead to conspicuous success: experience, meticulous attention to detail and a combination of keenness and perseverance. He thinks that women are more likely to have these qualities than men. A hundred years earlier, the great Kelson simply commented that 'ladies delight in salmon fishing after the fatigue of London gaieties, and hardly ever give it up once the taste is acquired.' It's not London gaieties that wear me out but I take his point and I don't think that women should be put off by the attitude of some men.

In any case, despite male protests, angling is an activity in which sex differences to do with strength are irrelevant. There is no need for a ladies section in angling, it equals things up between the sexes. Timing is more important than brute force and before modern, lightweight rods became available, women wielded nineteen foot Greenheart salmon rods weighing three pounds. And the term angling is not gender specific either - a real rarity these days.

Another way in which angling equals things up between the sexes is in relation to the clothing worn. At the most basic level, neither sex can find spending a penny easy when wearing chest waders but, more generally, the notions that a fat man is portly whilst a fat woman is a disgrace are diminished by angling clothing. Funnily enough, breeks suit everyone whilst trousers don't suit a lot of women and everyone looks the same in baggy jackets. Wearing a buoyancy waistcoat makes everyone look like a Michelin man and as the hat tends to hide whether you are a man or a women you have a chance for some anonymity. Not that individualism is denied. There is plenty of room for eccentricity or style. Lady Cox sports a silk scarf when angling whilst Diana Rigg wears a most becoming cowboy type hat.

And there is the added bonus that there is no annual diet for the sun drenched holiday. No more worries about slimming down to fit a bikini and bake yourself a pale golden brown which will not be seen by anyone when you get home. Unless, that is, you want to walk around in a chilly English summer with your blouse tied rather than buttoned. No, after an angling holiday, you will return with very brown hands and face - perhaps a little extended up the arms if the weather has been particularly hot. Just enough for colleagues to admire. Of course you will look a little odd undressed as the rest of you will be quite white but then your husband will look exactly the same.

Any other advantages?
Lots actually. Not least of which is the habit of angling hotels to be superior without being overpriced. Isaak Walton's companion commented favourably on the clean white linen, smelling of lavender, and it is nice to think that some things, at least, haven't changed for the worse. Any angling hotel which hopes to keep its reputation knows that comfort and good food are essential after a day on the river so you always get a drying room - they know that you will have wet things - lots of hot water, a good bar: what an American guide we spent time with in the Catskills referred to as the mahogany ridge (the only place where the fish get bigger and success is assured) - and excellent food.

You can, of course, eat as much as you like as you will work it all off the following day. Although relaxing, game angling is extremely strenuous. And, because you have been in working gear all day, most guests make an effort to dress up in the evening so you can transform yourself from the sexless angler into an evening woman. It's rather nice really because you get to eat your cake as well as have it. Not that the dressing up is all that formal. Comfort always comes first so it is not unusual to see a male angler coming down to dinner, bathed and polished in a well cut suit and bow tie but wearing slippers on his tired feet.

The company is usually good too. Whilst you do find some all male groups with the inevitable boasting and jockeying for position, this is the exception rather than the rule. Most experienced anglers are modest, unassuming people. The experience of angling ensures this as they have long learnt that they only have to prove things to themselves. The 'rules' of conversation are interesting too. The angler who goes on and on about the monster fish that was lost (I have not yet heard anyone admit to losing a small fish) soon gets discouraged by the listeners.

And it is not done to boast too much about one's successes - one must wait to be asked how one did or for a complimentary comment if your fish is lying glistening on the slab in the rod room and it is expected that you will not bore people too much with the details. In fact, beware of boasting about your first salmon as traditionally you are expected to treat all the anglers in the hotel to champagne. This accounts for the one bad habit of angling hotels - they invariably mark up champagne dreadfully.

So, you can talk about your fish a little and commiserate with others a lot. You can expect to give and receive advice freely and your mistakes and blunders are acceptable topics of conversation, especially if they involved you in getting wet, stuck in a tree or generally looking rather foolish. Name me another situation where men freely talk in an amusing but self-deprecating manner? It all tends to make for pleasant evenings after arduous days on the water with the added bonus of displaying yourself as a modest heroine.

And, I cannot underestimate the sheer bliss of being an integral part of the countryside. No ordinary naturalist can ever see quite as much wild life as an angler. You could sit in a bird hide uncomfortably for hours without seeing half as much as you will on a river. As it is vital to angling success that you look inconspicuous and move quietly, and because you are usually in the water performing what appear to be routine movements with your rod, you quickly become accepted as part of that environment.

And then you really see the most marvellous things. Some of them are fairly accessible to any quiet watcher, such as swans performing their mating dances or sailing angrily down river with neck arched and feathers puffed out to warn off another male wandering onto established territory. Others are little less than miracles. I was angling quietly when a red necked grebe paddled confidently past me with her babies in tow. Yes, I know that the books say that red necked grebes don't nest in this country but any angler will tell you that most of the naturalist books are quite inaccurate and seriously under-estimate the variety of wild life in this country.

I have seen ospreys where they are not recorded but I'm not telling where. They are getting along quite nicely without a team of naturalists erecting defences for them and people coming to stare at them, so it will remain my secret. Anglers, too, are the people most likely to see otters. They are not as rare as many make out but, again, why should I tell? My reticence seems to be working quite well for them at the moment. Seeing an otter peeping at you with its eyes like a pair of spectacles over a slightly worried expression is the most wonderful experience, one that will take your mind completely off the fish but one you will treasure for ever.

Not all the sights are tranquil. I hate to see mink around the water and am convinced that we should not allow any more 'foreign' animals into the country because of the upset they cause to the delicate balance of nature. Grey squirrels too, are not such charming creatures. I saw one harassing a mother duck with twelve little striped fluffs of babies and was sorely tempted to intervene as the mother duck rushed in and out of the water to fend off the predator.

The flowers, too, take on a different dimension when you are angling. If you go regularly to the same water you get to watch the season unfold and become quite involved in the whole process. What never fails to surprise me is how trees have a wonderful sense of timing. Whatever the weather and despite people's complaints that spring is slow or fast in coming some years, I have noticed that large trees always unfold their leaves in the same week each year. At the risk of sounding a little like a bit-part in a Jilly Cooper novel, I feel that I have missed something important if the flowers have moved on to their next stage whilst I have been away from the river. Going angling means taking bird and flower books along too and you quickly learn which are the most accurate and how limited our knowledge of our own countryside is. My favourite flower book allows for me being an idiot - it classifies flowers in a very simple way: white, yellow, pink and blue flowers. Much easier than most wild flower guides which presume that you will have an idea of basic botanical principles.

All these natural things are important but the fish are the most important of all. They are sensitive creatures which only thrive if the rest of the ecosystem is operating well. The water needs to be clean, the insect life abundant and the weeds just right. So if the fish are in good condition you have a good feeling that the world is right somehow, and I find that very comforting. If the fish lose condition or die then, equally, I know that I should be protesting somewhere about pollution.

Another advantage of angling for married couples is the enhancement of the relationship which a shared activity brings. Don't believe all the rubbish you hear about men going fishing to get away from everything (the inference being their wives but it's probably the children really). Angling is not really a solitary activity. Very few anglers like to be truly alone on the water as it is more companionable to share one another's successes and failures. I find it a great pleasure to walk quietly up a field after a day on the water, tired but inwardly satisfied and knowing that my husband feels the same way. No less a pleasure is total agreement about how holidays are to be spent and knowing exactly what to buy him for Christmas.

And most men agree, although I am not sure that I would have fitted the bill for Cholmondeley-Pennell's plea made a hundred years ago: 'How charming it would be when we sally forth after breakfast to lake or stream, to have the companionship of a "sweet girl graduate," who with hair either golden or otherwise, would by her graceful companionship double the pleasures of success! There would be no slovenly casting, no calling a halt for pipes or liquor when the fish were on the rise . . . how much pleasure, now lost to most of us, is gained by the man whose wife takes heartily to fishing. In this way she becomes not only his helpmate at home, but his "chum" and true comrade when on his rambles by flood or field.'

Disadvantages?

I must be honest and admit that there are some difficulties for women anglers even if they aren't exactly disadvantages. Not least is lavatories. Of course, there aren't any for women anglers and you can't stand close into the hedge like men do. Probably because of this, it is not a subject which is addressed much in angling books although Hugh Falkus' book on salmon fishing does contain one useful piece of advice - he recommends any angler setting out for the day to take some lavatory paper.

It's not too bad if the water is heavily wooded but some exposed lakes and river banks do pose a bit of a problem. One stretch of the Tweed where I fish regularly has not even a little bush. I did tentatively suggest to the senior ghillie, Kenny Jack, that perhaps I could donate a small rhododendron for planting on the bank but abandoned the idea after my husband burst out laughing and said that a Lebanon Cedar would be needed for me. However incommoded women anglers are, they can take heart that it is not just their problem. Men don't always have it so easy, as one chap who went salmon angling in February with his thermal, one piece long johns back to front would tell you.

The only way to tackle this problem is to face up to it and get rid of any false modesty. Why shouldn't women be allowed to relieve themselves in semi-public as men are? Just give other people a chance to turn their backs. I would be interested to know how women skiers cope as I always think it must be even harder for them with the all-in-one garments and the wide expanses of pure white snow.

A problem for me is cows. Unfortunately, almost all stretches of good water seem to have very wide fields alongside, invariably occupied by huge herds of large and energetic cows or bullocks. And it is not as though you can walk smartly away from them, as getting to the water's edge in waders, carrying a rod, net and bag, slows one down enormously. The judicious use of a wading stick can be helpful but I swear that cows know when you are afraid. They always seem to follow me and one angler of my acquaintance who waded into deep water to avoid a curious cow found that it swam after her.

With time, I have got less afraid of cows and learnt that bullocks are less of a threat as the season goes on. They seem to settle down after they have been out in a field for a few weeks. Having a dog with you is disastrous as cows will always follow a dog but dogs and angling don't go very well together anyway - you won't see anything very wonderful if you have a dog poking about the water's edge.

Bulls are a different matter altogether. It is worth finding out if the area you are to fish is likely to be bull country. Bulls are much more common than they used to be. I'm not sure why but it does seem that artificial insemination is less popular. I am assured by most people that bulls are quite harmless except when angry. I would find this sort of statement much more comforting if I knew what made bulls angry. It is worth remembering that there is no such thing as a dangerous bull any more than there is any such thing as a dangerous rottweiller. They are both quiet, lovable creatures until they do something - and then what they do is so awful that they are promptly put down.

I have been advised that when faced with an irate bull one should step to one side in the manner of a matador and slip one's wading stick through the ring in its nose. Hmmm. And then what? I have been face to face with an irate bull and I have no desire to repeat the experience, even though it did lead to my only experience of walking on water. I crossed a deep, fast flowing river without even getting my feet wet. I can't remember how I did it but the terror remains vivid. So, I reckon that the presence of a bull is a strong contra-indication for angling.

I think that bulls are about the only thing that would put me off angling. There is lightning of course, not very sensible

. . . I crossed a deep fast flowing river without getting my feet wet.

to carry on if your rod is made of carbon fibre. But, by and large, I think that disadvantages are there to be overcome. Angling, I suspect, is a bit like pregnancy in that women experience both more positive and negative feelings about the whole thing than men. Think of it this way - you may suffer more discomfort but your pleasures equally will be more keenly appreciated.

Why a book for women?

In many senses this book is entirely redundant. Juliana Berners said it all five hundred years ago. What she said then still holds good. For example, she said that salmon take a floating fly in warm water and a sunk bait in cold water although male anglers think that this is a relatively recent discovery stemming from lengthy, logical argument. And, she manages the whole in thirty-six lively pages.

So why don't I simply recommend her excellent treatise to you? Well, it is not that accessible. There is one copy in the Bodleian library which you can't take out although you can wade through it on microfilm in most library reference rooms. There is a nineteenth century facsimile copy and the book has been rendered into modern English - but by an American man.

There are some modern angling books written by women. Joan Clarkson gives a wickedly funny view of male angling 'rules' and there is an excellent angling diary written by a woman - Muriel Foster's *Days on Sea, Loch and River*. Most angling diaries are dull affairs, full of boring details about water heights, flies used and catch sizes but Muriel Foster's contains the barest details and the most brilliant watercolours depicting the lochs she visited, the flies she used, and a lovely illustration of herself in the rain. I recommend it most strongly. It doesn't tell you how to set about angling though.

There are hundreds of 'how to do it' books. As I mentioned earlier, the English have a curious compulsion to write about their angling. I like a lot of the old ones but most recent offerings are pretty tedious affairs, full of technical detail about everything from which knot to use, the parabola of the cast and how to judge the angle of the sun for maximum catching. I never could tie knots from illustrations and I haven't a clue what a parabola is so, unless you like technical books, I wouldn't recommend that you start with them.

My rationalisation for this book is that there is no book written in a womanish way. I don't profess to know much about angling and I am certainly not particularly proficient but I do enjoy it and have some idea about the particular problems for women in getting started - and that's what this book is all about. As any woman starting angling is going to be exposed in every move she makes and very likely hampered by unsuitable equipment, I thought a few hints might prevent the keen beginner avoid the self-fulfilling prophecies which seem to beset most women when they have a go. So many wives try angling only once and get discouraged because they never have a reasonable chance to get off the ground - rather like trying to learn water skiing with your whole family watching: undignified and doomed to failure. And I would like to see more women on the waterside. It might reduce the number of comments about 'do you fish too?'

CHAPTER TWO

GETTING STARTED

Essential planning

Angling, like most things in life, is made a lot easier if you happen to have a reasonable husband. Though if you haven't one you shouldn't necessarily be deterred. You can always do a Shirley Valentine. Simply find a friend and set off to a hotel which offers tuition. In fact, even if you have a reasonable husband, this might well be the best way to start as you can make your mistakes in front of someone who will not be able to bring them up later. You need to make sure that the tuition is carried out at a place where it is usual for there to be women beginners. For example, the Altnaharra Hotel in Sutherland offers 'Ladies First' weeks where guests all eat together but women go off with other women and the men have to take 'second fiddle.' Courses are regularly advertised in all the angling magazines and there is no reason why you should not write for details before committing yourself. A quick flip through the angling magazines will show you that it is not unusual for women to be involved - the Voss Barks, for example, run a hotel and angling courses in Devon and Arthur Oglesby, perhaps the best known salmon angling instructor around at the moment, owes much of the credit for his fame to the competence of an old pupil - his wife, Grace.

Although I made my tentative trout angling beginnings on the river bank with my husband as mentor, I really started salmon angling at the Half Moon Inn in Devon. We had gone for the trout but a sudden spate brought a good run of salmon into the River Torridge and the proprietor, Charles Innis, sent out all guests who were ambulant to have a go. Like most places, he willingly loans equipment - even waders sometimes - and gives lessons. It is a bit unhinging having a lesson from Charles though. It never lasts longer than twenty minutes as he maintains that he can tell in that time whether or not you have the capacity to do it. And, at the end of the twenty minutes he is too polite to tell you whether you fall into the 'hopeless' or 'natural' category!

If you do start with your husband as teacher, it is worth putting in a bit of preparatory work. Half the fun of angling is in the tackling up stage, deciding what fly to use, what tactics to adopt and how many fish you are about to tempt. And nothing is more boring than standing idly by whilst your husband has to set up both his own and your rod. Even worse, is the frustration he will experience if he has just started angling himself and then has to break off every five minutes to help you get out of tangles and put on new flies.

So, if you make the decision to start, practise assembling a rod and tying flies before you set out. You can practise casting if you have a big enough lawn but I haven't found this particularly helpful as it feels entirely different when you try it on the water. Better to spend the preparation time in handling casts (the fine bits of tapered nylon attached to the end of the main line) and tying a couple of basic knots.

Beginning angling is not something which is best done on a spur of the moment. It really won't do to turn up on the waterside with your husband and expect to get started or arrive at a hotel and think that all you need to be taught is how to cast. Preparation will make a good deal of difference to your first attempts - to both your comfort and sense of achievement. Nowhere is this more obvious than in the clothes you wear.

What sort of clothing?
A woman having her first taste of angling stands out a mile. Anxiously trotting behind her wadered and green-jacketed

husband she looks as though she is dressed for a day in the garden or walking the dog. Already, she is looking a little cold and harassed. And it will get worse. Basically, don't think that you can set out in your old trousers, anorak and wellingtons. For a start, your head will feel the cold. Even on the hottest and stillest of days, there is usually some sort of breeze on the river and more often than not it is channelled the length of the river in a cutting gale, nipping your ears and whistling through your hair.

You will also be lifting your arm to cast, a movement which even in the most economical of dry fly anglers will mean that your arm is stretched and your neck exposed more than in any other activity except tennis. And, in salmon angling, which is a two handed job, both your arms are waving about. It is pretty obvious that the average woman's anorak will be neither long enough, nor roomy enough, to accommodate casting movements. Not only will the wind whistle around your hatless head but a sneaky draught will creep round your waist. This is when you find that your jumper is too short and that your trousers aren't cut quite deeply enough to allow you to bend and stretch (those who have already moved to elastic waisted trousers, skip on). To add to your discomfort, your trousers are probably by this time coming out of your wellingtons, the inadequacies of which will be apparent as soon as you try to move in the water.

Wellingtons are only of any use on open banked reservoirs, as wading, even in the shallows, causes the water to splash up and you will then use most of your concentration peering anxiously at your legs to make sure that you are not getting wet. The sensation of water trickling remorselessly down your socks, inevitably to soak your feet, is one to be avoided at all costs. If it is a warm day and you are not too cold, you will soon be frustrated as you realise that the fish have moved into the deep and inaccessible water to avoid the sun.

Even worse, if it is a good angling day - dull and wet - you will be cold and exposed. Your hands will soon become not only cold and wet but the rain will be trickling down your neck and up your wrists. You need to think warm and comfortable before setting out on your first trip and plan accordingly. Other sportswear might solve some of these practical problems, particularly hiking or sailing gear, but even this is not quite suitable as the colours will probably be too bright. Success in angling requires that you take on the appearance of a bush as far as possible. This is the real reason why men affect such strange attire when angling. The old rugby shirt, the ancient jacket, the battered old hat, have little to do with eccentricity and a reluctance to part with old clothes and much more to do with feeling comfortable and appearing inconspicuous on the water.

Until about a hundred years ago, anglers used not to wear special clothes but the prominent writers of the last century soon advised otherwise. Francis Francis commented:

'With regard to dress, some people are inclined to ridicule

. . . positive black or white or anything that glitters or is unusual should be eschewed.

the idea of there being any necessity for attending to it at all. I am sure, however, that excellent grounds exist for not being too conspicuous in this respect. The trout is very gentlemanly, and does not like 'loud dressing;' positive black and white, too, or anything that glitters or is unusual, should be carefully eschewed, particularly on the upper and more conspicuous part of the person. A tall black hat, or one of the genus called 'shiner,' I do not recommend; and though I would rather fish in the Bishop of Winchester's stream than in his lordship's company when in full canonicals, I should equally consider Mr Chadband in his cerements an objectional party for successful trouting on a shy or well-fished stream.'

Women were given similar advice, the most notable being Kelson who laid down the law with as much detail on clothing as he habitually did about every aspect of angling. According to him, the proper attire for ladies included:

'... light, warm, tweed dresses, skirts to the ankle, loosely fitting coats and blouses, stout Balmoral boots with low, broad heels and soft felt or tweed hats to match their dresses. A high-legged pair of porpoise-hide boots and thick woollen stockings are usually deemed sufficient, as, if a fisherwoman must get wet, she will soon walk herself dry again.'

His book has a distinctly bossy tone but his daughter plainly didn't take him too seriously as photographs show her in a natty boater and a well cut costume. I can't quite make out if she was wearing porpoise-hide boots but she certainly managed to wield a heavy looking rod and, although accompanied by a ghillie, had the burden of carrying her own lunch. As her father remarks:

'... it would be awkward to want food or drink on one side of a stream with the attendant carrying it on the other.'

At least he recommended a flask of sherry or claret, so women anglers of years gone by might have had to walk their wet feet dry, but at least they had the consolation of a throat-warming drink.

I don't hold with this wet feet business at all and reckon that you might as well start with a pair of waders even if you balk somewhat at the expense when you are not sure if you will continue angling. It is a big outlay (the cheapest waders advertised for mail order in angling magazines start at around £21) for what might be a single trip but why not try to borrow a pair from the smallest man you know and fill up the space with several pairs of socks? At least you will have some confidence about approaching the water and getting somewhere near where the fish are lying. If you do invest in a pair of waders, it makes sense to spend a few pence on a wader repair outfit. At its simplest, this involves a tube of glue and works well for urgent repairs after you have caught your leg on some barbed wire. Even the tiniest hole leads inevitably to that wet, trickly feeling and the knowledge that the day will be spoilt by a sodden sock. It is worth appropriating an old jacket from your husband. A large jacket is a great comfort for the beginning angler as it will cover your hands when it starts to rain - you can turn the cuffs back for casting. Also, should you get thoroughly miserable or tired and your husband doesn't want to pack in just at that point, the jacket acts as a sort of tent if you sit down on a stone or tree stump, covering you completely and sheltering you from winds and rain. Also, the big pockets mean that you won't be burdened with a bag slung across your body and digging into your shoulders as you get tired. Plus, it makes you look more anonymous and you will not draw attention to yourself. The last thing a beginner wants is to be watched and nothing causes people walking along the river bank to stop and comment more than the sight of a woman angler. Passers-by are a nuisance at the best of times. They tend to stand quietly for ages and then comment: 'I don't know how you can do it, seems pretty boring to me.' They, of course are doing nothing. The ideal is to look as unassuming as possible, to give the impression of being sexless. In this way you will get the privacy to carry on angling without being assessed to see if you are any good.

An acquaintance of ours who regularly wears a baggy jacket

and an old flat cap of her husband's continued angling one afternoon after her husband had decided to pack in for the day. As he packed his tackle away in the car boot, he commented to a fellow just about to start that he would have the stretch all to himself. The newcomer glanced across the field and replied 'apart from that old fellow with grey hair.' Her husband swears that it is the first time he has had the opportunity to crack the old line 'that's not an old fellow, that's my wife'.

Most of your other clothing can, with thought, be adapted from existing stock. Any long baggy shirts and jumpers will do and lots of thin layers are better than single bulky items. Women's trousers are not terribly comfortable as they are not usually cut with enough generosity at the waist and have to be laboriously wrapped round the ankle to fit into boots. Breeks are easily the most comfortable to wear and you can cut down a pair of trousers if you don't want the expense of buying new breeks. The sort with elasticated waist bands are the best and you just cut off the legs to about calf length and turn them up to make a hem to accommodate an elasticated garter. This gives you lots of freedom at both waist and leg level and allows for women's bodies being periodically different in dimension. A pair of knee length socks should be fairly easy to purloin if you don't have any already. Lots of paper hankies and a waterproof hat and you should be ready - or almost.

It sounds ridiculously obsessive but it really is worth having a spare set of clothes in the car - a 'falling-in' kit. The problems involved in falling-in and getting dry don't tend to come home to you until it actually happens. But when it does, it is more than a minor nuisance. I remember only too well trying to dry off a soaked husband - he had fallen in completely. Emptying the waders is the first thing (no, they don't drag you down, despite all the scare stories they actually aid buoyancy) but on that occasion we found that all we had in the car boot was a little towel used for the dog and a spare tie!

We promptly added spare trousers, shirt, socks and a large

towel after that incident. However, the next accident was me. I did a prat fall at a local reservoir when I slipped on the greasy yacht launching strip. I was soaked to mid-waist and rather shaken. I disappeared behind a wall to dry off as best as possible and forced wet limbs into my husband's spare pair of trousers, tying them up with an old tie of his. I emerged from behind the wall to find him talking to another angler. 'Can I introduce you to the president, darling?' I heard him saying and I presented a damp and bleeding hand. In films, women always manage to look quite attractive when they have got wet; towel twined fetchingly around the head with a few damp tendrils of hair escaping, the oversize clothes of the hero failing to hide the womanly curves of the body. But I looked like a bedraggled tramp recently dredged from a canal. Since then, the boot of the car has always contained two plastic bags labelled his and hers. They contain everything - knickers, the lot. And they have been used several times by both us and friends.

Later on, if you become addicted to angling, you can start to add extras. A wading stick is useful as it gives women more confidence in the water but is just another hindrance in the early days. You feel festooned enough in the beginning and it takes long enough to work out where you are going to hang your net. This is quite literally a thorny problem and you soon get used to the first law of angling which says that nets get entangled in trees and hedges at the slightest provocation. This is just something anglers get used to eventually.

Angling in cold weather is not impossible if you set out well equipped. As mentioned earlier, a too large jacket is a positive boon and so too are moleskin neck ties (easier to wear and warmer than ordinary scarves). Keeping your hands warm is more difficult. Woollen, fingerless gloves are pretty useless as they soon get wet and cold and cut off the circulation to your fingers. Mittens with fold back tops get stuck in everything. On really cold days I use a pair of sheepskin shooting mittens which keep the backs of the hands dry and warm yet leave my fingers free for casting. If you are a poor swimmer or nervous in fast flowing water, don't listen to all the people who warn against waist or chest waders. They are fine - and you can sit down on wet banks in them - but you could invest in a buoyancy waistcoat.

These are warm too. They are guaranteed to hold up a fifteen stone man. I don't know if this is true as fortunately I haven't had to test mine yet. For the more affluent, there is a short jacket made of Gortex with an inflatable life jacket inside.

If you really get smitten with angling you will soon want the proper gear. Home made breeks do for a while, especially as a comfortable pair is difficult to obtain unless you are a standard sylph. Breek makers seem to have adapted men's designs and simply offer women similar pairs in what purport to be women's sizes. They never seem long enough in the leg for me or wide enough across the beam. I have found that a stylish and comfortable pair is best obtained from a ladies section of a men's outfitters. Here you get the experience in making breeks combined with a sensitivity towards women's shapes.

There is a sort of inverted snobbery in angling attire; an aspiration to look thoroughly well worn yet basically well cut. The answer is to buy the best clothes you can afford and wear them like fun so that they soon look suitably battered. The pinnacle of achievement is to have an ancient Barbour jacket which has been extensively renovated. To wear a new one is to look like a posh dog walker. And the snobbery is grounded in common sense, you do want to be comfortable and unhampered. So, if you are going to wear a pair of hunter wellies, the first thing to do is to cut off the straps - they will only get entangled in your line. I haven't quite managed to decorate my hat with flies though. I can never get them out once they are in and, anyway, I long ago settled for a waterproof, rather than a woollen hat. The wool and tweedy ones shrink. Don't worry about being vain about your angling clothes, there will be enough mortifying experiences on the river bank to induce in you a suitable sense of humility.

What sort of equipment?

A beginning angler is not only spotted by the hopeless inadequacy of her clothing for the expedition but also by the fact that she is usually to be found on the edge of what her husband considers to be an easy pool and that she is half-heartedly brandishing a rod of antique proportions - not a beautiful spilt cane rod which is probably her husband's pride and joy but some old thing with bent ferrules, the whippings coming undone and a reel which does not quite match up and contains an ancient line with cracks and weak spots.

This is not because husbands are intrinsically mean and thoughtless. It is simply that if you have not put any serious thought and preparation into the trip then your partner and mentor probably won't have either. And he won't want to risk the possibility of having any of his precious tackle damaged. He will have found you a rod which he never uses himself. This in itself is a good reason for not taking it. If it is one of his mistakes then it probably won't do for you either. Where he puts some thought into the matter, he will probably be guided by the single fact that you are not as strong as he is and he will have hunted out a light, soft action rod on the mistaken assumption that this will be easier for you than a heavy or stiff rod. Any old reel will have been provided although he well knows that balance between rod and reel, and a matching line, are essential.

He probably thinks that you won't catch anything first time - a fair assumption as you should be prepared to have several fishless days in the beginning unless you are beginning on a particularly well stocked reservoir with ravenous trout which have been pellet fed and are in the habit of swimming towards anglers in the hope of being fed rather than taking the more natural course of avoidance. This is the reason why he puts you in a pool which looks easy and then sets off up river to enjoy his own sport. It is unreasonable to expect him to stand by your side for the whole day if the fish are on the take, so, if he has taken his own rod with him, don't expect too much in the way of attention. All the more reason for starting at a hotel with proper tuition.

The problem with 'easy' pools is that they are so easy to cast over that every passing angler has a couple of casts and as a result the pool will contain hardly any fish at all or only the shyest of fish. Therefore, easy pools are invariably the hardest pools. The beginning angler thus gets the hardest pool at a time when she has no ability and is hampered with the most unsuitable equipment. No wonder many women only try it once.

It might sound sensible to start women anglers off with soft, light rods but this is an inaccurate assumption. In fact, it is easier to begin casting with a stiffish rod. This is because a high degree of proficiency is required for soft action rods. In inexpert hands they just flop around and the line does not travel far. They are too fine and delicate. What you need is a cheap, medium-firm action rod rather longer than your husband's if he is the same height as you. This will enable you to lift the line and place it on the water with some accuracy. And you need to be able to do this if you are to gain any confidence at all.

All my trout rods are heavier, longer and firmer in action than the men I go angling with would advise. This is because they advise from their own experience, and they are mostly expert casters who appreciate light rods with a whippy action. The first rod I ever used was light and soft in action and I spent hours of frustration trying to cast against a wind with no success and finding my reactions were slower than the action of the rod. A firmer action means that I have more control over what I am doing and I can get more distance - important when you have not yet gained the confidence to wade deep.

The reel is important too as it must match the rod. On a holiday with tuition you will get the chance to try out different rods to get the feel of the right one for you. This is not easily done in a shop where you can't practise the actual cast. Also, I think that it is helpful to start with a weight forward line. There is much to confuse and muddle the beginner about lines. They come in all colours because argument rages about which colour is least likely to be seen by the fish, and different types. The tip can be tapered (single or double), weight forward (which means that it is heavier at the tip) or you can get one with a shooting head. For Spey casting for salmon you must have a tapered line and most dry fly purists (more about them later) would not be seen dead with a weight forward line but the extra weight at the tip helps the line go forward, roughly in the direction you were aiming for. It might not be the line you eventually settle for, but at this stage when you know nothing at all about the differences between various lines, a weight forward line is just the thing to get you off to a good start. If, of course, you are a naturally gifted athlete with wonderful co-ordination, you can use anything as your ability will overcome unsuitable tackle.

Part of your preparation should, therefore, involve you in persuading your partner to lend you a long enough rod with a firmish action and a reel which matches the rod. If he is making this sort of sacrifice, the least you can do is go to a tackle shop and buy your own line and some flies. The rod will be marked with a number which tells you what size line to buy and most shops will put the line on the reel for you. This not only keeps your husband happy but saves you from angling with an old frayed line which will catch on the rod rings and hamper casting. You can get a decent line for about five pounds although the better ones start at around ten pounds. It is worth remembering that a good line is the only link between you and the fish. Whilst you are buying a line, you could do worse than buy a few extra casts so that when the inevitable tangle happens you can quickly tie on a new cast, popping the tangled one into your pocket. It will be easier to sort out in the dry comfort of home.

It is important to have your own flies, not only for the independence this will give you but also because the choice of fly is such a personal thing. You always feel most confident with a fly which you have chosen. Flies are funny things. It is well known in angling that flies catch more anglers than fish. They are irresistible in glass covered boxes in the shop and every beginning angler has a tendency to buy the pretty, bright ones although eventually you will probably settle for a collection of dowdy looking things, well chewed.

Lots of men tie their own flies and swear that there is no satisfaction that compares with catching a fish on a fly you have tied yourself. If you have neat fingers, a lot of spare time and cash to burn (the basic equipment means that tying your own flies is not a cheap option in under twenty years) then by all means take up fly tying. Otherwise, start a basic collection in a tackle shop near the water where you intend to begin. You will receive advice on which sorts of flies are having success at each time of the year. Local advice is always worth having and you will also find that other anglers you meet on the water will be quick to give you flies when they find that you are a beginner.

It isn't quite the done thing to ask a fellow angler what they are using if they are catching and you are not, but a delicate probe on the lines of 'any suggestions as to what the blighters might be interested in?' will usually result not only in the necessary information but also a presentation of one which the angler has just tied up to add to your collection. Try not to use it straight away as it is very embarrassing when you lose it in a tree on your next cast and you can't quite remember what it was.

Eventually you will need a net, a wading stick and a priest - the lead-cored club which is used for delivering the last rites as swiftly and painlessly as possible. As all these things will only weigh you down until you get the hang of them - quite literally they hang about your person getting entangled with every twig and piece of grass you encounter - you might as well save them for later. If you do hook a good fish in your early days you can call for assistance or, as last resort, do an Isaak Walton. He reminds us that the hat can always be used for netting the fish. How wet you are prepared to get your hat will indicate how keen you are about angling and should be an early sign of total addiction. In any case, you would probably be able to beach the fish as you will no doubt have been put in a pool with a gentle shelving slope. If you hook a small fish, you don't need to bring it out of the water. Simply reel the line in until the fish is on the surface and then gently wiggle the hook between thumb and forefinger until it drops out of the fish's mouth. Any angler will tell you that this happens only too easily - usually when you don't want it to come off. A pair of medical forceps make this operation even more simple and this item is somewhat easier to cadge from an angling medic than the loan of a rod.

It is important to gain some confidence in wading if you are to enjoy your angling. This is not only because the fish are usually just beyond your casting range but also because it is easier to cast in the water - less snags behind you for your line to get tangled up in - and you are less obvious to the fish than you would be waving your rod about on the bank and casting a long shadow over the water. If you read the modern books on angling you are likely to be a bit put off wading because men talk endlessly about the need to wade deep in fast water, usually following this up with instructions on how to swim out with your rod intact after you have fallen in. I think they make a bit of a macho thing about wading and do it rather more than is necessary.

In any case, women can't wade as deep as men in fast water because of their wider hips and backsides. If you are in really fast running water, it is advisable not to go in too deep. If you are shaped at all like me you will find that your backside acts as a shelf and you find yourself being lifted up by the water. It is a most odd - and alarming - sensation to find yourself on involuntary tiptoe in fast water.

Also, it is well known that it is easier to wade into the water than wade back. This is largely because you usually wade downstream and then have to face the current coming back but also, sometimes, the water rises whilst you are actually angling, especially if there has been heavy rain some hours before. This is where a wading stick comes in really handy as it gives you a bit of purchase on the river bottom and something to hang onto if you wobble or slip on a stone. Wading sticks are a nuisance as they have to be tucked behind you whilst you are actually casting but their advantages outweigh the inconveniences. I use one which doubles up as a landing net. It is attached by a lanyard but has a spring clip so that the net part comes away quite easily when required. Unlike rods, these can be tried out in the shop so don't just buy any one without trying it.

Bags are nothing but a nuisance. If your jacket has enough pockets, then you can carry all the equipment you need. Special waistcoats are ideal as they are all pockets with even enough space to put any fish in the back pouch. My bag is usually left in the car with spare equipment but I do take it as far as the river bank if food is required. Food, whilst angling, is not quite as simple as an ordinary picnic.

Eating and angling

Game fish have the annoying habit of either being on the feed or the move at more or less the same time as people. Trout, for example, in the early and best part of the season, tend to feed at breakfast, lunch and tea time. Later on in the season, they feed mainly at dinner time. Salmon are equally irritating, tending to move at these times and then settle down quietly in pools after your meal times. This makes it extremely difficult to get a decent meal while you are angling. And you don't want to be weighed down with an enormous picnic basket.

This is a big problem if you think you are going to be the sort of angler who sets off at dawn and returns at dusk. Some men anglers do this. They are the grey and haggard looking ones. Unless you are a morning person, I think you might as well miss the first rise altogether. Much better to have a really good breakfast and amble down to the water mid-morning, feeling ready for anything. You can then fish on for a few hours before you need to think about lunch. This is no problem if you have a ghillie as he will insist on stopping for a meal, and very sensible too. The best thing to do is repair to the pub if there is one near enough, but the alternative is to take a small packed lunch which you can leave in the anglers' hut, if there is one, or on the river bank. I have found that a drink is more important than food when angling so if you are pressed for weight, settle for a couple of cans of coke and a few biscuits if you have to carry your own food. Kelson's claret is fine if you have a hut and can sit down to enjoy a proper picnic. An alcoholic lunch doesn't do much for your casting but it does wonders for your confidence.

After the tea time rise, I usually pack up. I have been angling

An alcoholic lunch doesn't do much for your casting . . .

for several hours and there is no point exhausting oneself. And, who wants to miss the evening meal in the hotel and the chance to find out how everyone else got on? If the weather dictates evening angling, usually when the weather is hot and the sun is bright on the water, then go out just for the evening - after you have eaten. You are supposed to be enjoying yourself and there is really no need to flog on all day until you are ready to drop. The fish will still be there the next day.

How much will it cost?

There is bound to be some expense. If you persist in setting off in your own clothes with borrowed equipment then it is likely to be expensive in terms of wasted time. By far the cheapest way of getting started is to go to a hotel. If you find that you don't like angling after all then it has cost you no more than any unsuccessful holiday, but your partner will have been able to carry on angling if nothing else.

If you start with your partner, then be prepared to pay for waders, a line and some flies. It is possible to buy a beginners trout angling outfit which includes a nine foot carbon rod, a matching reel with two spools, line and backing, casts, and 24 flies in a fly box for around £50. A longer rod for reservoir angling will cost only a few pounds more and the post and packing is less than three pounds. A beginners kit for salmon angling would be considerably more - about three times as much. Even if you invest in a salmon kit, the overall cost will be less than equipment for an average skiing holiday and, again, if you don't want to continue, there will always be people willing to take the equipment off your hands. Your angling husband isn't going to get upset about your giving him a new line and a box of flies.

If you do become addicted, then it will cost a whole lot more. You will gradually acquire a good deal of equipment and will have to pay for day tickets or club membership. As I mentioned earlier, this makes present buying a lot easier and I find it wonderful to open my presents with the knowledge that I am not going to have to feign surprise at finding food processors and such like. And it's not so expensive in the long run. The initial outlay may be heavy but angling holidays are the only ones where you don't need to budget for daily pocket money - you can't spend money whilst you are on the river bank.

It can get a bit expensive if you get flooded off and are stuck in a small town with nothing much to do. On such occasions, the town will be filled with tweed clad men, wandering around with a slightly bemused air on their faces. The tackle and clothes shops do a good trade. I take the opportunity to have breakfast in bed and a lie in, a habit approved of by most men anglers. Following the news that everyone was flooded off, one such asked my husband at breakfast where I was and on being told that I was in bed, he responded with feeling 'try to keep her there until lunchtime. It's early closing day and you will be all right.'

A cheaper method still?

All that I have mentioned so far assumes that you will be taking up fly fishing. However, a lot of anglers use flies which don't look even remotely like flies and, not infrequently, use what are loosely termed baits. There are several methods of bait angling, the most common one being spinning and the equipment needed for this is even cheaper still. Any old spinning rod and reel will do for a beginner although the spinners attached at the end are expensive, mainly because they get snagged up under the water surface and you lose them. A washing up liquid bottle is useful here (more of this later).

However, for some peculiar reason best known to their own irrational selves, men get very upset about bait angling. They do it an awful lot, especially for salmon, but try their best to deny it because they think it too easy and rather infra-dig. They get very heated about it and write lots of articles about when is a fly not a fly and try to occupy what they see as the moral high ground. In one hotel, where the guests had been catching salmon on spinning tackle, one disgruntled fly purist wrote in the catch record book 'consider the lilies of the field . . .'

I can't really see what all the fuss is about as lots of flies are indistinguishable from baits and sometimes it is just unsuitable to use a fly at all. Still, one should avoid upsetting established anglers' sensibilities (however irrational) and I think it is as well to start with flies if you are hoping for lots of help and advice - and if you want to be taken seriously. There is, of course, nothing to stop you learning how to use baits later and I will discuss some of them in the next section where I hope that I have whetted your appetite enough to start on a little salmon angling. If you intend to start with trout, skip a chapter.

CHAPTER THREE

SALMON ANGLING

Why start with salmon?

Dame Juliana Berners chose to start her book with salmon on the grounds that it is 'the moost stately fyssh,' but there are other, equally compelling reasons for suggesting that a beginning angler starts with salmon. Not least of which is that any fool can do it. As salmon don't feed in fresh water they cannot be tempted by a skilful angler into taking a representative of their current dish. You don't catch a salmon. It catches you. And the nice thing about it is that salmon have not been known to discriminate between competent and incompetent anglers. Neither do they always do what experts expect them to do. Although an experienced salmon angler will usually catch more salmon than most, there is always hope for the rank beginner who can reasonably expect to have a little luck. This does not happen with trout which are shy and crafty creatures, therefore there is a lot to be said for making a start where you are most likely to get some immediate reinforcement.

Another good reason for starting with salmon is that the technique needed is far slower than for trout angling and it is as well to learn how to cast in the slowest way. With a double handed rod, you have time during the cast to look round and see how your line is behaving. This gives you more opportunity to learn from your mistakes than you will have in casting for trout, where a quick glance behind would simply result in a massive tangle in the nearest bush. Also, that famous thing, the strike: that is, lifting your rod briskly as soon as you feel a fish take so that the hook will be set, is much slower in salmon angling. If you learn trout angling first you will have a lot of unlearning to do when you turn to salmon, as I found to my cost.

Even more convincing is the fact that salmon angling is mostly done in small parties in order to share out the costs. This means that you are more or less guaranteed a good time and there will be lots of other people to lend you equipment and give you advice. Also, you get the opportunity to try out lots of different methods. As mentioned earlier, although men like to say that they are fly purists, in practice they are much more eclectic.

To be honest though, these are the not the real reasons why I recommend you start with salmon. The simple fact is that it is the most exciting activity in the world apart from one other (and, if you are happily married, you are not short of experience in that area). Seeing a salmon head and tailing in the river, feeling the slow, determined take with the resulting weight on the line, wrestling with the sheer force and pace of a fighting salmon, netting the silver bright beauty at long last - it's brilliant. All anglers go on about it at great boring length. Entirely understandable and forgivable. Cholmondeley-Pennell explained it perfectly in 1889:

'The rise of a big salmon to your fly is electrifying in its effect. There is a moment of intense uncertainty and suspense as he disappears after having risen, and you are waiting the result . . . He has missed it! Your face is as pale as death, and you sit down unable to stand from sheer excitement. You have to wait another minute or two before you make another cast. All cares and troubles, all thoughts of everybody, even of the wife of your bosom, are cast to the winds during those glorious moments of uncertainty; your whole soul is bound up for the time being with the silvery monster you have aroused from his stronghold.'

Exactly. So you can see why you can't take up angling until you can send the children off elsewhere. Angling is between you and the fish and other people are there for supporting roles later - cronies and sympathetic friends. Responsibilities are not to be assumed during angling time. The ultimate freedom to be yourself, alone.

Not unnaturally, salmon anglers don't go around offering to share their opportunities to engage in this wonderful activity. A good deal of snobbery has arisen around salmon angling and it is generally thought to be expensive and exclusive. This is not necessarily true. Patience is the main thing which is needed and although salmon angling on the great rivers is expensive and difficult to obtain, there is much on offer elsewhere. Simply look at the advertisements in the angling magazines. They aren't offering the opportunities to catch huge bags of salmon but they are offering reasonably priced opportunities to catch the odd fish. In some places, salmon angling is free, especially estuaries and some Irish lakes.

There has been a move with the advent of farmed salmon to stock some lakes for salmon angling. Please don't go to one of these. They are foul and disgusting places where the poor fish are dumped just for sport. They have no chance to follow their usual migratory pattern and they quickly lose condition. It is akin to scooping goldfish out of a bowl. Whilst I have argued earlier that there is precious little nobility in angling as some people would assert, angling for salmon in these conditions ensures that there is no dignity either - for you or the poor fish. A fresh run salmon is a beautiful thing that should be respected. The best thing about the lovely creatures is that they are not at all well understood despite years of intense scrutiny.

Salmon lifestyle

Salmon are wonderful creatures which manage to have several identities during their lives - something I envy more than a little. They get a good deal of variety and no more hardship than most wild creatures. They start life as tiny parr in the higher reaches of rivers and streams. They feed ravenously and, if they are not eaten in large numbers by goosanders which herd them into shallows and pick them off (don't believe any of those stories about goosanders being rare - there are thousands of them), they turn into exquisitely silver smolts. Quite how they know when they should stop being parr is something about which we know little. But once a salmon becomes a smolt, it stops hanging around in the river and sets off towards the river mouth and the sea.

When it hits the brackish water of the estuary, it lingers a while waiting to get accustomed to the salt water. Then it heads off to sea, exactly where we are not sure, although, like Toyland, the salmon feeding grounds are somewhere off Iceland or Greenland. Here the salmon feed voraciously again and then decide to come back to the river to spawn. They do this at the age of one year sometimes but most salmon stay at sea longer and return as two, three or even four year sea water salmon. The older the salmon is, the bigger it is likely to be; although sometimes, when only a small number run the river to spawn, they are bigger than usual for that river. Some people think that this means that the sea feeding was poor for that particular group. When they enter the river they run in bursts of about three miles at a time, resting up in lies which contain rocks to shelter them and where there is maximum oxygen in the water. Spring fish tend to hang around in the river quite a long time whereas autumn fish are in somewhat of a hurry to get to the spawning grounds. Some autumn fish are still fresh from the sea but quite ready to spawn.

Salmon which have only been at sea for one year are called grilse whilst the others are called spring, summer or autumn salmon. From a catching point, none of this is very important. The ideal is to catch one which has come quickly into the river and still has sea lice on its body (again, these have to hang around a little while in the brackish water while they adapt to fresh water). This means that the fish is very fresh and full of oils. Not only will it look superb - the term you should remember for boasting later is 'like a bar of silver' - but it will be best for eating. The longer a salmon stays in fresh water the more its condition drops off as it will not eat once it enters fresh water. If it is a long time getting to the spawning beds because of being trapped lower down by low water or an extremely cold spell, it will rapidly become quite stale.

It is terribly important to know the difference between a fresh and a stale salmon. Firstly, you will ruin your reputation as a cook if you serve a stale, dull-looking salmon. Secondly, if it is near to breeding time, you are supposed to put it back. No more than you would like to be interrupted just as you get into bed with your loved one, neither should you disturb a ripe salmon. Some anglers maintain that it is all right to take a cock fish but recommend putting ripe hen fish back. I think it as well to put both back. It should not be too hard to tell as a cock fish nearing spawning grows a big kype (a jutting out bony lower lip), goes very red looking, becomes thin in the body and generally looks out of condition. The hen fish goes black-looking and is often full of eggs. These ripe cock and gravid hen fish are often referred to as 'kippers' and 'baggots.' It is really quite easy to tell whether a fish is fit to take but most anglers find that their ability to discriminate becomes dulled in direct proportion to the number of fish they haven't caught that week. Fish get prettier as they get rarer.

Never believe anyone who says that a stale fish will do for smoking. No fish improves with smoking and you get out of the smokery what you put in. If the fish has lost a lot of weight, there simply won't be much flesh to smoke. It might seem that you should just not carry on if the fish are stale but it is not that simple as salmon seasons overlap and you can be angling for autumn fish which are quite fresh and still catch the odd summer fish which has lingered awhile in the river.

Salmon which escape the depredations of netsmen, seals and anglers go on up the river and spawn. They then start to slip slowly back down the river where they become silver again and, if not too exhausted by the whole trip, go back out to sea and start the whole process again. These fish are called kelts.

It is the height of treason to take a kelt and doing so in some places will be accompanied by a firm request to leave. As no-one wants a kelt in the first place - they are quite inedible - this should not be a problem. However, the salmon learns little sense and is as likely to take your fly or bait on its journey down river as it is upstream. As I said earlier, you don't really have much say in the matter which is entirely in the hands, or rather the mouth, of the fish.

It is at times like this, when you can't be sure what sort of salmon you have hooked that you learn that there are lots of other names for salmon depending on which part of the country you are in. Early one spring, I hooked a salmon on the Tweed when I was with the famous boatman, Bob Patterson. As the fish ripped up and down the pool, I was praying out loud 'oh, don't be a kelt. Please don't be a kelt.' Bob kept trying to reassure me, 'its a fish all right.' I remained unconsoled until I realised that in Scotland, as a drink is a whisky so a fish is a fresh salmon. In other places, the names are different. For example, a grilse is called a peal in Southern Ireland, a name usually reserved for sea trout in England and Wales.

Everyone scorns an angler who takes a kelt so it is important to know one if you get one. This is usually easy as kelts tend to look exactly like you would if you had swum miles upstream for a bit of nooky - they are thin and bedraggled looking. But they do improve in condition as they slip back to the sea and many people have been fooled by a silver looking kelt. The best thing to do is to look at the size of the fish overall. A fresh fish has what is called a small head although what is really meant is a large body in comparison to the head. In angling, fat is beautiful. The other way of checking is to look at the gills. In a fresh fish these are bright red and clean whereas in a kelt they are darker and covered in grubs. Some people have told me that kelts are always cock-eyed but I think they might have been having me on. Being on the whole good-humoured people, anglers are great jokers.

Why are salmon so stupid?

It is impossible to say that salmon angling is a blood sport because they are not stalked in the same way as other fish. There is no effort made to tempt them to eat as they never feed in fresh water. For years, anglers refused to believe this although no-one has ever found anything in the stomach of a salmon. Some people maintained that salmon regurgitate food on being hooked and all sorts of silly things like that. Why they ever believed it in the first place is a mystery to me. It seems pretty obvious that a river which has several thousand large salmon moving through it each year simply could not provide enough food. It would be like trying to feed a herd of elephants at a vicarage tea party.

Even as late as the nineteen fifties one famous angler still maintained that salmon feed in the river: '. . . salmon do not feed because they need food, they feed like an overfed woman nibbling chocolates - because they like the taste, the goodies

. . . the goodies look tempting.

look tempting, and they have nothing better to do.'

Hmm. Strikes me that if that is all he knew about why women eat chocolate, then he was talking out the back of his head. Still, he caught plenty of salmon - as I said earlier, they don't discriminate between people. This is just as well as men have put forward some pretty stupid reasons for why a salmon takes a fly or bait when it is patently not feeding. This is partly because they want to make sense out of what the salmon is doing and partly because they want to seem scientific and rational themselves. Salmon constantly confound anglers by being remarkably fussy about what they will seize, responding to ridiculously large baits presented low in the water sometimes and at others taking a fancy to tiny little flies. One Scottish ghillie even hooked a salmon on a piece of orange peel.

I think this mystery is rather appealing and adds to the fun and uncertainty but reasons are still offered regularly. They range from anger, instinct, fear, curiosity, and hunger. One of the funniest and most confabulated theories is one put forward by a chap called Waddington. I love the cause and effect he argues. Basically he says that the salmon has:

'. . . the habit of hunting and seizing his food so strongly ingrained upon his nature that . . . he is unable to resist the habit of hunting even in the very different surroundings of the river, and it is this that causes him to take the fly. It is the force of habit and not fear, anger, instinct or curiosity that accounts for the one weakness that allows him to fall prey to the angler.'

Rivetting stuff but he then has to account for the fact that this 'habit' manifests itself in such peculiar ways. Such an ingrained habit should not be subject to this degree of fussiness that a salmon shows. He tries to account for this by suggesting that the habit is manifested in two ways which reflect the salmon's sea feeding pattern; the large baits being similar to deep ocean feeding for large prey whilst small flies remind the salmon of spring feeding in warmer, shallower waters out at sea. The fact that a salmon takes a bait in the river and returns to his lie is said to be similar to sea feeding, although there can't be any rocks in the ocean to make lies and we don't know whether salmon feed on the run in the sea or stay in one place. In fact, we haven't a clue what they do in the ocean. Waddington tries to cover up all these weaknesses in his argument by talking about 'dualities' reflected in the salmon's sea and river life.

All we do know from several centuries of studying salmon is that they feed voraciously in midwater in the ocean, and in the river are more likely to take a large bait deep down in cold weather and a smaller one nearer the surface in warm weather. They are more likely to be caught when they are getting ready to move from one lie to another and after they have just moved. As far as anyone can tell, their movements are dictated by the weather, by the air pressure and by the time of day. They always seem to know when it is about to rain. Some people maintain that the taking times are related to dusk and dawn whilst others lay more importance on the tidal movements.

This 'knowledge' is only outline knowledge as salmon are always ready to make a fool of you by doing the opposite of what you expect. I have my own theory about why salmon take. I like to think that it is sheer bad temper. I imagine a shoal of salmon waiting offshore for the water to get to the right height and then making their way upstream in runs and stops, rather like townspeople taking their annual holiday and setting off up the motorway to the seaside. Salmon tend to stop in a suitable pool after a longish run or when they meet some obstruction like a waterfall or a sudden drop in the water level which strands them temporarily. This seems just like human motorway behaviour to me, similar to motorists getting frustrated after traffic jams and going into a service station for refreshment. I reckon that salmon get just as annoyed as we would if we were interrupted in the middle of a well-earned break in a long important journey or just as frustrated by crowding and impediments.

Just another silly theory. That's the beauty of salmon angling: we don't know much about salmon behaviour so we can all hold forth with our pet theories. And it is just as well that we don't know as our ignorance is the best safeguard the salmon has for its survival. If we really knew exactly where they went at sea and what they ate, then they would pretty soon be trawled out by huge fishing boats. Mackerel fleets already catch quite enough salmon accidentally.

How to encourage a salmon to catch you

If you can afford to book salmon angling on one of the great Scottish salmon rivers, then it is quite simple - read John Ashley Cooper's book on the subject and then take the local advice available to you. However, you are likely to start more modestly and it does help to have some idea about the basic methods people regularly use. In salmon angling, these methods are more diverse than most men would admit. Broadly speaking, there are two main methods - bait and fly - but both categories leave scope for a lot of variation.

Bait angling is most commonly done via spinning. In this you attach a metal spinner which looks something like a small fish, and throw it out with the rod and line across the water. It is derisively known as 'chuck and chance' and considered to be too easy for a talented male angler to bother with. In men's books, the authors usually say that they used to spin for salmon but no longer have any desire to resort to such easy tactics and then rave on about the beauty of casting a fly for salmon. Do not be taken in by all this. Even the most prominent salmon anglers are regularly to be seen 'chucking' a spinner across a river although they do tend to keep quiet about it.

Why do it then? In the first place, it is the most sensible way of persuading a salmon to catch you when the water is high or dirty. Secondly, although it is an easy way to get started, it is more complicated than most people make out and there is a good deal of skill in getting it right. The spinner has to travel across the water just in front of the salmon's nose and you will need to fish your bait at the correct depth, correct speed and with the correct size of spinner.

This means that you need to know how deep the water you are casting across actually is. In cold weather, you are aiming to put the spinner slowly across the water to the salmon which will be lying low down. This means that you have to work out just how long your leader (the piece of nylon attached to the main line) should be. This leader is attached with a swivel so that the spinner will in actual fact 'spin' and you will need a weight to make it sink. Don't worry about the possibility of poisoning a swan with lead weight as many weights nowadays aren't made of lead at all and even those that are, are too round and heavy to constitute a hazard to swans. If you break your tackle and lose a weight in the river, it will sink like as stone to the bottom. Swans do not feed at the bottom of deep pools. Their necks are not long enough.

It is advisable not to lose your tackle as spinners and weights are expensive. As heavy spinners easily get caught on under-water snags, it is as well to be armed with an old washing-up liquid bottle. When well and truly snagged you attach this with the nozzle to your line and let it float out across the river altering the angle of the snag. Then you give a sharp tug and usually the whole tackle comes easily away from the snag. Try not to lose the washing-up bottle - this would not be environ-mentally friendly.

It is best to start spinning under tuition but the main points to remember are that you cast across and down the water and wind the spinner slowly back upstream when the water is cold. The colder the water and the deeper the fish lie, the slower your retrieve should be. As the water warms up, you use a smaller spinner and retrieve rather more quickly. When sum-mer comes and the fish are more lively, you can try spinning upstream.

This involves casting your spinner directly upstream and then winding the handle of the reel as quickly as you can to make the spinner travel faster than the flow of the water.

Salmon will often chase a spinner in this manner and the take is breathtaking. The spinner stops dead as though you have hit a large rock and then all hell breaks loose. It is most exciting.

Some men say that this is unfair as there is a big chance that you will foul hook a fish (that is hooking it accidentally in some part of the body other than the mouth). Foul hooking is to be avoided and ranks on a par with sniggling - definitely not the done thing. If you should do it by accident, you must always put the fish back. I don't think that you will foul hook a fish by this method as the fish is moving to your bait and it would be difficult to drag the spinner across the fish's body acciden-tally as it would be against the lay of the scales. However, this method is banned on some rivers so do check.

You can also spin with a preserved sprat. This is a bit messy as you have to push a long, fat needle with a vane at the end through the sprat and then tie a variety of hooks round its body with fuse wire. And it isn't easy to get the sprat to spin nicely in the water. Also, if you hook a salmon with a sprat, you have ruined your bait and have to start the whole process again. It is also a light bait compared with a metal spinner and not as easy to cast to the fish if there is a strong wind. It is funny to see the cast sprat twirling in the air like a helicopter as you vainly try to cast it across a wide expanse of water in a strong upstream gale.

Spinning is not the only way of bait-angling for salmon. There is also worming, prawning and shrimping. Prawning and shrimping is considered the pits by most anglers who regard it as most unfair and many rivers simply do not allow it. The reasons against it are that such baits spook the fish and/or are so deadly that they are unfair. I don't see the logic of these arguments as they can't both hold up. And I'm sure that if it was actually deadly then lots more people would do it.

It seems most sensible to prawn or shrimp for salmon when conditions are extremely difficult - when the water is too low to present a fly or when it is too dirty. My main objection to it is that prawns and shrimps are difficult to get on the hook. The needle which holds them on the hook has a nasty habit of going into your finger instead. Also, they are preserved in salt and sting your fingers as well as making them a funny colour. If you get round to attaching a prawn or shrimp to your hook then there are several ways of proceeding. You can cast across the river and let it roll gently across the stream but this needs a very light tension on the reel and makes the strike complicated. You can let the bait into the stream and then lift the rod tip from time to time in what is called a sink and draw method. This is all very well but you do tend to get a good deal of weed attached to the bait and this has to be removed between each cast and it is all too easy to remove the legs from the shrimp at the same time. In very low water, you can use a float in the same way that coarse anglers do but this is pretty boring.

All in all, prawn and shrimp angling is not too exciting, gives you few opportunities for boasting later as everyone will disapprove of what you have been doing (especially if they have had no success) and is pretty messy so it is best reserved for days when there is little alternative. Another method of bait angling disapproved of by so-called purists is worm angling. It is considered too easy to be worthy of the accomplished angler. In reality it requires skill and is extremely exciting. Most people who disapprove of worming simply can't do it.

Worming is best kept for difficult conditions such as high, dirty water. Experts say that water which is beginning to fine off after a flood is ideal for salmon catching but it can be difficult to assess quite what is happening when the river is very full. As a rule of thumb, avoid going out if all the swans and ducks have left the river for the safety of the fields. When they return, then you can start angling. Worming is also a sensible method to use on hot days when the water is low. This adds to the excitement. It is particularly suitable for the learner who has been unlucky enough to have been given a rotten spinning rod. A worming rod needs to be shortish and fairly stiff. You thread nice fat worms which have been kept clean (scoured) in moss. The easiest way of getting worms is to thrust a garden fork into a lawn and then tap the handle. For some obscure reason best known to themselves, the worms come to the surface. They are then threaded onto a long, hooked worming needle and the correct weight is attached a little higher up.

You then take the bail arm off the reel so that the line is running free and hold this with one finger before casting the worms slightly upstream. It is vital to keep your finger lightly on the line or else your line will disappear down stream at a rate of knots. With the rod held well up and your finger hooked over the line, you let the worms travel slowly downstream until you feel them bumping on the bottom. At a moment which feels right to you, you let them 'sit' and wait for a salmon to try to catch you. This is where it gets really exciting and you will need all your powers of concentration and patience.

Salmon rarely attack worms. They play with them. So, with luck, after a few minutes you will feel a bump-bump at the end of your line. It is vital that you do nothing as you have to wait for the salmon to swallow the worms. This can be very difficult because if you wait too long, the worms will just be removed and you will have neither fish nor worms. So, you wait with each bump-bump on the line on your finger and the bump-bump in your chest and then make up your mind. Having decided to go for it, you reel in the line quickly to get in contact with the fish and strike like mad (that is, lift your rod firmly backwards). Either battle commences or you are left feeling silly as the whole thing comes away in your face. It is a cat and mouse game which needs strong nerves. It is one of the most exciting ways of catching salmon and does not deserve to be run down by other anglers. If you catch salmon like this, always smile at your detractors - remember, they probably can't do it. If there is an angling record book at your hotel, the euphemism for worm is 'blackbird's favourite' or 'garden fly.'

All this said, I have to admit that there is nothing quite like taking a salmon on a floating fly. It is still called greased-line angling although modern lines no longer need greasing to make them float. For this, you need a salmon fly rod and line and have to learn how to cast. It is more difficult to cast a fly than a spinner and a salmon rod needs a two armed-action: you pull backwards with one arm and push forwards with the other - and you have to learn to cast off both shoulders. Because of this it is better to learn to salmon cast before trout casting which is done with one arm. Casting involves using the resilience of the rod to lift the line off the water, throw it behind you and then propel it forwards onto a chosen spot on the water. Apparently, the only action you need to learn in preparation is that of slowly but determinedly lifting and lowering a hammer.

In real life it is more complicated as the fly has an uncanny knack of flying off into trees and bushes and I find that the

. . . the fly has an uncanny knack of flying off into trees . . .

line has a talent for skipping with itself making knots in the line. There are also complicated salmon casts to learn such as roll casting and spey casting - this latter is for angling in places where there is no room for a back cast because of high banks or trees. These are best learnt under the tuition of experts as the technique is far too complicated to explain in a book. If, like me, you do not have natural co-ordination, then spey casting is best learnt with a tutor who has learnt to duck as your fly drops unaccountably and heads straight for your mentor's ears. Paul Gibson, now ghillie of Inchmarlo on the Dee, once threatened to arm himself with a plastic bucket to cover his head when I first started spey casting on the Tweed. Also, I find that one's ability to cast comes and goes. Sometimes I think I have really cracked it and the line goes out nicely each cast. Then a fish shows and I get all excited and my casting goes to pieces. It also disappears with tiredness and it is always worth having a rest or packing in early if you get tired - even if you have paid for a full day. It is better to enjoy yourself and do it well than struggle on when things are not going well.

Using a fly to tempt a salmon is not as straightforward as it might seem. As mentioned earlier, salmon don't feed in fresh water so there is no point in trying to imitate natural flies. Well known salmon flies owe more to their creators' flights of fancy than any living creature. As a general rule, use small flies and a floating line in warm weather, increasing the size and changing to a sinking line or one with a sinking tip in colder weather. Sunk line angling usually involves a fast sinking line and a large tube fly - coloured hair (often clipped from the nearest dog's or cat's tail) glued onto a tinsel-covered copper tube. This equipment is very heavy. The line takes a lot of lifting off the water as it sinks quickly to the bottom and the tube fly takes some casting so it is not advisable to start salmon angling in cold conditions. The main consolation for beginners with sunk line angling is that at least no-one can spey cast tidily with a four inch tube fly. Just how different a heavy tube fly is in the water to a spinner is an interesting point but one which the purists carefully avoid mentioning.

Salmon are funny creatures and will take anything from a tiny, single hooked fly, which would be considered small for trout to a six inch piece of plastic and metal which wobbles in the water. It all depends on the water temperature, the air pressure, and the mood of the fish. Salmon are completely indiscriminate and have been known to ignore a perfectly presented fly yet snatch at a bait trailing accidentally in the water. Experts will explain all about the need to control the 'drag' of the fly as it travels across the water to allow for the speed, or lack of speed, of the current but this doesn't always matter. I have a method which I call the 'Milner method of uncontrolled drag.' I use this when I make a particularly poor cast and the fly lands with a plop, surrounded by coils of loose line. It has been my happy experience on some occasions to find that a salmon has taken pity on my pathetic efforts and straightened the line out nicely, saving me any effort other than persuading it to come to the net. The main thing to do is to take lessons and remember to do the whole thing as slowly as you can - taking lots of time. This is particularly important when a fish takes hold of your fly. Allow it time to take some slack line and turn before moving your rod and it will hook itself. If you strike too quickly it is likely to come off. Also, no-one ever told me when I started that a hooked salmon almost always hangs quietly for a minute or so before it starts to protest. I had imagined that it would be action from the word go. However, you need to stay quiet yourself during this period and it does give you a moment to collect your thoughts and perhaps move to a better position to play the fish - that is if you can still breathe and your heart has not jumped out of your throat.

The only time this doesn't apply is in South West Ireland where the water is always warm because of the gulf stream. Here you should do everything more quickly as the salmon are mostly on or near the surface of the water. I learnt this particular lesson the hard way, persisting with traditional salmon angling methods for too long - despite good advice from Vincent O'Sullivan, boatman in Waterville, Co Kerry. It is always best to take advice from the local anglers, however odd it may seem, and be willing to discard the usual accepted wisdom. Conditions vary enormously and local people do know best. Local anglers know their water inside out and are much better placed to inform you of the most likely methods than an all round experienced angler whose experience is scattered and lacks detailed knowledge.

Also worth remembering for women anglers, is to keep the rod tip well up when playing a fish. Actually, mostly the salmon plays you and you have to follow its lead, but it does help to maintain control if you keep the line tight and pressure on the fish by using the length of the rod. To do this you need to play a fish by putting the butt of the rod firmly in your stomach so that the fish doesn't pull the rod down when it makes a run. This isn't exactly comfortable but is worth persevering with. Also, it is important to know which fish to put back and to do this carefully so that they are not damaged. The problem seems to be that kelts are always well hooked.

Cooking salmon

Having a salmon catch you and fighting with it as it plunges around the river - or even worse, decides to do nothing but hang there like a stone - is excitement enough but salmon angling has the added pleasure of an edible end product. I never cease to be amazed at the number of friends whose disapproval of my angling melts away when there is the chance of a side of smoked salmon. Catching your own salmon soon makes you choosy about the quality of the fish you eat. If you take a salmon in poor condition, no amount of fancy sauce or careful cooking will make any difference to the end product.

Keeping your salmon fresh is always a problem on angling holidays, especially if you catch on the first day, so it is easiest to have your salmon smoked. Wherever salmon are to be caught, there is always a smoker and most will post fish on to you. Lots of anglers get very neurotic about smoked fish and are convinced that the smoker will slip them an inferior fish in the process. If you look round a smokery you will see that this is not true - the fish are carefully labelled. I have found that a reputable smoker will always advise on whether the fish is suitable for smoking as there is little point in paying for the smoking of a fish which has lost so much condition that there is little flesh to smoke. Having your own smoked salmon in the freezer is great.

Salmon under six pounds in weight don't smoke well and if you catch a small salmon in particularly good condition it is well worth taking it home in a freezer bag to cook whole. Restaurant salmon are usually about six to eight pounds and it is worth remembering that the average domestic fish kettle will not cope with anything much larger so don't try taking an eighteen pounder home to cook in one piece.

We have tried most ways of cooking salmon and find that a fish kettle is best if you want to have a salmon cold and whole. Simply put it in the fish kettle (or in foil in a large pan of water), bring it slowly to the boil and switch off the heat immediately, allowing the fish to cool in the water. Whatever the size of the fish, this method works perfectly as long as the pan is large enough to hold the fish comfortably.

A fish kettle is not so satisfactory for cooking a whole salmon to have hot as the kettle covers more than one burner on the stove and it is difficult to keep the water at the necessary lightly bubbling stage. After much trial and error, my husband maintains that the *Good Housekeeping* recipe works best. I haven't actually tried this but it works for him. Simply butter the inside of the fish and scatter parsley inside before wrapping it in foil. Then place it in the oven at 180°C, 325°F or regulo 4 and allow a quarter of an hour per pound and an extra quarter of an hour. Although not entirely traditional, we like a mousseline sauce as accompaniment. Details of this, and one or two recipes for people who have caught and eaten enough salmon to want a change from the plain, are listed below. If you still have to catch your first salmon, simply skip this section.

Mousseline sauce (this is a Constance Spry recipe)
3 egg yolks, juice of half a lemon, 3 oz butter, half a gill of double cream, salt and pepper.

Break the yolks into a bowl, add half the lemon juice, seasoning, and a nut of the butter. Whisk over water until quite thick. Take off the water and work in the softened butter, add the rest of the lemon juice and the stiffly whipped cream. It can be put back over the water if it gets too cool but does not really keep so make it fresh - your guests can wait for it.

Salmon steaks (a Michael Smith recipe)
Steaks of fresh salmon at least one inch thick, orange juice, fresh ginger, olive oil, pepper.

Marinate the salmon in a mixture of orange juice and olive oil with grated fresh ginger to taste. You need to be quite heavy handed with the ginger unless you have a particularly good palate. Grill the salmon quickly, basting with the rest of the marinade. Curl the skin off with a fork just before serving.

This is another dish which needs eating immediately. Better done for lunch as it will ruin whilst you eat a starter.

Potted salmon (another Michael Smith recipe)
1 lb middle cut salmon, 1 teasp powdered mace, 2 glasses Madeira, 1 tablesp chopped parsley, 4 oz butter, squeeze lemon juice, seasoning, clarified butter to cover.

Skin the salmon and cut into broad, diagonal slices, starting at the centre of the backbone and cutting to the outer edge. Arrange slices of salmon in layers in a fairly narrow, deep oven-proof pot, dotting each layer with a little butter, mace, seasoning, parsley and lemon juice. Pour over Madeira and cover with buttered paper. Cover tightly and bake at 160°C, 325°F or regulo 3 for one hour. Allow the dish to cool, remove the paper and strain the juices into a small pan and reduce (take care that you do not end up with burnt butter at this stage). Pour the liquid back over the salmon and then put a plate and weight on top. Put in the refrigerator to set, then cover with clarified butter. This dish is not as fiddly as it sounds, it keeps well and slices up to serve six people for a generous starter.

Salmon with a walnut crust (a Julian Morby recipe)

2 lb salmon (tail piece), 3 oz walnuts, 1 bunch watercress, 1 tablesp Dijon mustard, 1 tablesp clear honey, 1 tablesp olive or walnut oil, seasoning, and walnuts and lemon for decoration.

Place the skinned salmon in a roasting dish. Finely chop the walnuts. Wash and dry watercress and chop finely. Mix walnuts, watercress, mustard, honey and oil together. Season well and spread on the surface of the salmon. Bake for 25 minutes at 200°C, 400°F or regulo 6 or until the crust is lightly browned.

It is important to use the tail piece for this recipe and a middle cut for the potted salmon as the tail piece is the best bit of the salmon, holding more oils than other cuts. The middle and head piece can be a little dry.

Salmon roulade (a Pool Court recipe)

First make a brandade with 1 lb salmon by adapting any brandade recipe - there is a good one in Robert Carrier's *Great Dishes of the World*. This is the easy bit as long as you remember to leave out the garlic.

Sponge recipe: 3 large eggs, 2 oz plain flour, 3 tablesp glycerine, 3 tablesp chopped parsley, half oz salt, pinch sugar, seasoning.

Place the eggs, salt, sugar and glycerine in a warm bowl. Whisk until frothy and the froth holds in light peaks. Put sifted flour, seasoning and parsley in the centre of the mix. Fold by hand very gently, turning the mixing bowl slowly at the same time. Lift onto a swiss roll tray that has a well greased and floured, greaseproof lining. Bake at 160°C, 325°F or regulo 3.

The base of the sponge tends to stick to the greaseproof lining but gently brushing the back of the greaseproof with cold water helps it to peel off. Cover with brandade mixture, roll up and chill. Serve in generous slices.

This is a super recipe although very complicated and fraught with difficulty at the sponge mixture stage. I used to make it a lot. However, it usually gets eaten quickly and no-one ever asks how you managed to make a sponge without sugar which is most mortifying after all that effort. So, I now tend to make do with smoked salmon for starters.

CHAPTER FOUR

BROWN TROUT ANGLING

A gentle art

In complete contrast to the salmon, whose river life is filled with urgency to move upstream and whose eating has long ceased, brown trout are completely preoccupied during the catching season with eating as much nourishing food as possible with the least possible energy expenditure. They are cold, calculating eating machines with excellent eyesight which lie facing the current of the river but sheltered from the force of it. They lie almost motionless, looking for food to float down the stream towards them when they will then make a lightening move to grab it before returning to the lie. Sometimes they bask in the sun but mostly they do very little.

We know quite a lot about what trout eat - not least because Kelson's father made him lie in cold water watching fish from below. He was a remarkably compliant child, even by the parental standards of his day. After finding his first attempt was hindered by muddy water and his inability to lie still, he practised in a clearer but colder pond year after year. He commented that 'the penalty I paid for my underwater investigations was a slight deafness, which affects me still.' What his mother had to say on the matter is not recorded.

Another intrepid investigator of that century carried out tests to see which food caused the most rapid growth in trout, comparing tanks of trout fed on worms, grubs and insects. The insect-fed trout easily outgrew the others and this is why trout are most likely to be found in the clear, swift flowing reaches

What his mother had to say is not recorded.

of rivers with abundant fly life. The delicacy and sensitivity of trout to their surroundings makes them good indicators of river quality and their absence from a stretch of water is as good a guide to the quality of the water as any sophisticated laboratory testing.

This means that trout feed mostly on, and just under, the surface of the water. However, when the water is running fast and dirty after heavy rain, they grub about on the bottom eating whatever goodies are carried down the river. They also like to live in deep holes under tree roots at the edge of the river where they can eat grubs and such creatures which drop from the trees. Very big trout become cannibals, preying on their smaller brethren.

The sort of water the trout inhabits and the food it eats affect the colour of the flesh and its flavour. Trout from slow moving, muddy water actually taste muddy and the large cannibals are almost inedible. Rainbow trout (which are not indigenous to this country like the native brown trout and are usually in lakes and ponds) taste the best of all. This probably accounts for their popularity with fish farms. I think that the speckled brown trout is much prettier than the brilliant rainbow with its stumpy tail but no doubt the rainbow is pretty when reared in its native North American habitat.

Basically, brown trout feed at intervals during the day when there is a fly hatch, which begins low down in the water. The insects rise ot the surface where they rest a while and then dance in the air, mating, before they fall back onto the water as a spent spinner. Trout eat them at all three stages of development but the rise of the trout to spent spinners is most spectacular with the fish leaping out of the water to grab a fly or swatting it with its tail. Trout also eat a lot of other insects such as midges which they do with a light sipping action which is often called smutting. When you can't catch rising fish, it is customary to say that they are smutting. This might or might not be true but is a recognised and acceptable excuse for angling failure. They also do things which annoy anglers greatly, such as spending most of May eating stone fly nymphs low down in the water and steadfastly refusing the anglers' offerings. Anglers are afflicted with a strange parallel response to rising trout. As the sight of a succulent insect on the water surface tempts the trout, so the rise of the trout to the insect tempts the angler whose behaviour can become quite irra-tional - especially when the trout are rising prolifically in what anglers term a 'boil.'

I can remember vividly one summer evening when my husband and I took a visiting Canadian friend to our local reservoir for a gentle evening session. As we parked the car and looked across the flat expanse of water to judge the ripple and see if the rise had started, we were astounded at the activity. Instead of the occasional plop of the odd fish taking the first of the spent spinners, the water was alive with trout swatting fly after fly and their gulps were clearly audible.

The effect on us was immediate and ridiculous. Not a word

was spoken as we began to tackle up with an indecent haste which more than matched the dinner scene in the film *Tom Jones* for pure greed and desire. We stumbled ludicrously to the edge of the water and began thrashing madly with rod and line, desperate to take part before the boil ended suddenly as we knew it would. We none of us hooked a single fish but became more and more frustrated as the trout continued their greedy, flamboyant feast - taking flies only inches from our offerings as we continued with longer and more desperate efforts. We were sure the greedy fish would make a mistake sooner or later and we never paused to stop and think.

We were being stupid, heavy handed and greedy. And we paid the price for such behaviour. We ended up fishless, tired, frustrated and ill at odds with ourselves. Whilst salmon angling calls for slow, deliberate activity needing perseverance and determination to gain the reward of a heart-stoppingly exciting battle with a magnificent fish, trout angling requires more deft and gentle movements with guile and stealth - even when the fish seem to be feeding indiscriminately. The rewards in trout angling do not involve the immoderate passion of salmon angling. Rather there is the quiet satisfaction and pride of having worked out how best to approach this shy fish and deceive it against all its sharpness of eye and caution of life style.

Trout angling is considered a gentle art which demands the careful presentation of a fly on or in the water to deceive the trout into thinking it is like the fly currently being eaten. It cannot be rushed or done with loud movements as trout are easily alarmed and they cannot be tempted to eat when their natural food supply is not on offer so you have to be patient and wait for the fish to start feeding before you can start. You have to forget your own thoughts and think fishy ones if you want success and therefore as an exercise in patience, it is extremely salutary.

As Isaak Walton said, it is: 'A rest to his mind, a cheerer of spirits, a diverter of sadness, a calmer of unquiet thoughts, a moderator of passions, a procurer of contentedness, and that it begot habits of peace and patience in those that profess and practise it.'

I think it is important to remember this and not be lured by the 'science' of many angling writers' advice. Developing an obsession with the technicalities of the velocity of casting or the exact replication of the emerging insects distracts from the development of a oneness with the water, a feeling of rhythm and contentment which is much more rewarding than a constant striving to extract the maximum fish from the water on each outing.

Scientist or artist?

Whilst obviously a trout angler must approach the water with some degree of stealth, this can be carried to unseemly lengths. The author of *Fine and Far Off*, H R Francis, set an excellent maxim for all trout anglers but he was rather extreme. Faced with an exposed stretch of river with suspicious trout he cast from the confines of an adjoining ditch. He cast unsighted, feeling rather than seeing the rises. Impressive stuff until he describes what happened next. On hooking a fish, he had to scramble out of the ditch and rush towards the river. He concedes:

'I ought in frankness to admit that with more fishable water within easy reach many anglers would have thought the success hardly worth the pains it cost. This was certainly the opinion of a dear old friend and fellow sportsman who witnessed my first sortie from the trench and landed my first fish for me. He laughed until he cried at the figure I cut in scurrying towards the bank, and could never afterwards be induced to exhibit himself in the like undignified position.'

No, the maxim of 'fine and far off' for me means not always the finest line or the nearest ditch. I follow H R Francis in general but have no desire to imitate his feats of agility. And I have no desire to imitate exactly the fly upon which the trout are feeding. Trout anglers fall into two schools as far as choice of fly goes, with one set striving for exact replication and the other setting more store by presenting the fly in a tempting fashion. I prefer the second option but mainly because I am woefully ignorant of the details of fly life in the water and am completely unable to tie my own flies.

It doesn't really matter which position you adopt but it is useful for the two schools of anglers to avoid each other. The replication enthusiasts do things such as carry little nets like those which children use for stickle-backs and dredge the water so that they can examine the fly life before they start. They also carry long handled spoons and when they have caught a fish they scoop out the contents of its stomach so that they can see what the trout has been eating. I have never been able to follow the logic of this. It always seems self evident that you know what the trout has been eating if you have actually caught one but it seems to please the people who need to know that they exactly imitating the fly of the day.

The reason the two schools of anglers should keep apart is simply that they will never agree and will only irritate each other. This is a bit of a problem if your host is of the opposite school of thought to yourself. This happened to my husband and me in Devon one year. We had played host to a dear friend (but replica addict) and annoyed him by offering only general advice about what sorts of flies generally did best. He was quite appalled at our ignorance of the more subtle details. On our return visit to his water, we were ambling along the bank enjoying assessing the runs and rocks and looking at the weed and trees as we decided on likely spots when our host sprang into the air, right arm extended. He opened his hand triumphantly and told us exactly what sort of spinner he had captured. Saddened by the paucity of our fly boxes (as presentation enthusiasts we had only a few well-worn favourites with us), he kindly took us home whilst he tied us perfect replicas. We have them still because the rise was over when we got back to the river.

A technical approach to angling holds little appeal for me -

probably because I am not technically proficient generally - but also because much of the detail of it is extremely dense and abstruse. I used to read avidly in my early angling days, keen to pick up any information which would improve my ability, but finally gave up after struggling unsuccessfully to understand the finer points of light and shade. Consider the following advice from an angling expert (Pearce, 1981):

'It seldom happens that an angler casts a shadow directly in line with his cast. Fortunately, it often falls at a pronounced angle to the flow of the stream, and if this angle is in the other quarter from that in which he wishes to fish then he has a larger sweep of water available. An angle of 45 degrees in one direction will give him 90 degrees or more in the other, with every possibility of success.'

I studied this repeatedly and still couldn't make sense of it. Especially as, at that stage, I was still very tentative about wading anywhere above my knees and unable to lay a line gently enough onto the water to tempt anything but the greediest of fish. So I came to the conclusion that subtleties of light and shade could wait until I became more proficient at the basics. In the meantime, I developed the habit of retiring to the river bank to sit down quietly when my casting was going badly and there made the marvellous discovery that sitting quietly and watching the river gives one quite enough information to catch the occasional fish.

Insects emerging from the water or flying over the land drift lazily across your vision so that you can decide on whether a change of fly is needed. Any regular rise of a larger fish is more easily noted. You make the astonishingly simple discovery that one of the best indicators that a hatch is starting, and therefore the trout will start feeding just under the water surface, is the presence of swallows and pied fly catchers darting along the water, making rapid swoops to snatch up a fly. So, when the swallows are high in the sky, continue to sit down peacefully enjoying the scenery. When they come down, wade out slowly - avoiding the sharp rocks you have spotted from your vantage point on the bank - and start casting the fly you have decided upon as you sat there looking at the insect life. Swallows are only to be found in the summer months but seagulls often behave in a similar manner and can be good indicators of feeding fish. Much the easiest and least stressful way of angling.

But all this enthusiasm about relaxing into the atmosphere is not getting you started. As a rank beginner, where are you going to fish, what flies are you going to use and what can you do to make the first trip a successful one? There are many different types of trout angling but, roughly speaking, male trout anglers seem to fall into two main groups. There are those who have access to the finest chalk streams teeming with fat trout rising regularly to abundant fly hatches in gin clear water. These anglers are dedicated to dry fly fishing with soft action, cane rods and the finest of lines which they cast out with the greatest of delicacy, delivering the fly like gossamer in front of the trout. This sort of angling is reckoned to require advanced skill, cash and connections. You are unlikely to have any of these as a beginner so the second group of trout anglers will bear more useful scrutiny for your aims.

Other male anglers start at different points on what seems to be a continuum along the road to total addiction to trout angling. Here, a start may be made in coarse fishing with the angler then moving to reservoir or lake angling using lures which are fished low down in the water. These lures are supposed to represent small fish and other aquatic creatures but I suspect represent the fly tier's fancy for using peculiar materials. They are the most extraordinary creations made of fluorescent thread, tinsel and suchlike. They have peculiar names too such as 'dog nobbler' and 'babydoll.' I always think that they look like the results of occupational therapy undertaken by deranged but technically brilliant craftsmen. I have a totally irrational dislike of them, mainly because day-glow pink doesn't fit my romantic notions about trout angling but this has never stopped me using some funny lures when

. . . deranged but technically brilliant craftsmen.

salmon angling. Lures do attract fish.

Sooner or later, most lure anglers transfer to wet fly angling and then move on to river angling, or begin to get interested in dry fly - either on reservoirs or rivers - and develop a peculiar obsession with only using tiny flies. Eventually they too become dry fly purists about which there is a great deal of snobbery. More of this later, suffice it to say that this metamorphosis of the male trout angler is a masculine mystique. It is better not to try to plumb the irrational depths of the male mind. Men are funny creatures, as no doubt you already know. First you have to decide where on this continuum you intend to start. As you want to make your first trip a successful one - in terms of comfortable casting if not actually getting a fish - I would suggest that you start on a reservoir or lake if you do not have access to a good river.

Reservoir and lake angling

In order to thrive, trout need particularly clean water with a plentiful supply of oxygen. They are usually to be found in the higher reaches of rivers classified by the National Rivers Authority as A1 or A2 although sometimes they manage to survive in B1 and B2 rivers but then they taste as poor as their environment. Water of the A category is becoming more scarce due to pollution and water abstraction. This means that good trout rivers are expensive and/or exclusive unless you are a member of an angling club. As trout angling is immensely popular, the stocking of reservoirs and the making of lakes from gravel beds has come to the rescue of the ordinary angler of limited means. Whilst some reservoirs are horrendously expensive, it should be possible to find one which will not break the bank in terms of a day ticket, is reasonably near home and has sufficiently easy banks so that wellingtons will suffice.

A beginner would do well to avoid the large, famous reservoirs. Many of these require boats or detailed knowledge of which banks are the best. And they are likely to be populated by technically proficient male anglers standing close together - the last audience you want as you make your first feeble attempts at casting. Probably the best place for a beginner is a small lake, stocked with rainbows on a 'put and take' basis. This is a system whereby anglers purchase day tickets and report their catch at the end of the day. The proprietor then promptly pops out to a stewpot of waiting rainbows, nets the number equal to the ones taken by the anglers and empties the pellet-fed fish into the lake for the next day's anglers. Larger lakes and reservoirs usually stock on a two weekly or monthly basis.

It is not really angling because the fish don't get time to acclimatise and start feeding naturally or develop a shyness of people. Deprived of their comfortable, pellet-fed existence, they are quite likely to swim towards you. Still, rainbows are not natives of this country, rarely breed in British water and have a much shorter life span than the brown trout so you might as well catch one to eat as buy a farmed one at the fishmongers. They have the advantage for the beginner of taking voraciously which reduces the irritation of the brown trout's tendency to pluck at the fly and let it go. Rainbows also fight fiercely so you will quickly learn how to play a fish - keeping a tight line is easy with rainbows as they charge off madly keeping the line tight for you.

A small, open lake or reservoir is an excellent place to begin casting. There will be 'hot spots' where the fish are most likely to concentrate their feeding but as rainbows cruise around in lakes you can choose any bank from which to cast. It is usual to cast into the wind to get the benefit of trout feeding on land insects which are blown onto the water but it is much easier to cast with the wind behind you so, first of all, choose your casting position according to the prevailing wind. Also, bear in mind that it will be easier if there are no bushes to catch your fly on the back cast and no weeds in the water in front of you to pose obstacles as you retrieve the fly. If there is a soft piece of ground into which you can drive the handle of your net, so much the better. This is really a salmon angling habit for large nets but is useful for the beginner in trout angling who has not mastered casting without the added encumbrance of a net flopping around the body. The line has a tendency to get entwined around it and it takes practice to learn to unclip it and elongate the handle. Also, left flat on the bank, a net is easily mislaid.

Using the fly recommended by the proprietor - he will probably have a stock for sale - you are now ready for casting. Simply pull some line out from the rod and let it hang in the water. Then lift it into the air with a smooth backwards movement and propel it forwards onto the water. Lengthen the line a little with each cast until you have as much line out as you can lift and throw comfortably. Retrieve it with your other hand, experimenting with short, sharp pulls and more slow, gentle ones but try to keep the line tight enough so that you can feel if a fish takes the fly, at which point you should lift the rod tip sharply to set the hook. However, you will probably be so surprised with your first take that you will forget to do this.

Your instructor or companion should stand at your side advising you during this process. Most instructors tend to be too helpful and give too much advice, especially about what you are doing wrong. I find it more helpful to be told what I am doing right as casting is impossible if you are hesitating at any stage. Your line should travel behind you in a straight line which then loops upwards and comes back over your shoulder as it comes forward onto the water. As you can see what is happening in front of you, ask your instructor what is happening behind where you can't see. Advice about whether your line is not going far enough back or is dropping too low is the most helpful in learning how to cast.

If you do get into a fish, keep your rod tip up, hang on and pray. Then you can begin to bring the fish towards you with the line in your left hand. This is not as difficult as it might seem. I once offered my daughter my rod on our local reservoir when the fish were feeding well, and she was immediately into a fish which she played competently. As I approached with the net, she said in dismayed tones 'its started wriggling again, it feels funny.' She had hooked a second fish on the dropper fly. Netting two fish, struggling in different directions, is not simple, so start your angling attempts with a single fly. Also, this reduces the chance of wind knots in the cast. As nylon casts manage to knot themselves effortlessly in the slightest breeze, you should check regularly for wind knots. If you do have a knot and it has pulled tight, an ordinary pin is the most useful way of easing the knot sufficiently to undo it. The knot will leave a kink in the nylon but this can be smoothed out simply by stretching the nylon tightly over your wellington boot and rubbing it briskly across the rubber. If you don't attend to knots, you will have a weak spot on the nylon which is likely to break when a fish pulls.

River angling for trout
Having put in a bit of practice on your local lake, you should

soon be ready for trout angling at its finest - wild brown trout in a river. Try to avoid a river which is stocked with rainbows. It is one thing having them in enclosed lakes but they are pollutants in rivers. As grey squirrels have driven out red ones, so North American rainbow trout take the food of the natural brownies and affect the balance of life of a river. Fortunately, most stocked rivers have abandoned the practice of stocking with rainbow trout and have returned to brown trout although there is some worry that the particular genetic stock may not be quite right for each river.

The choice? Well, it depends where you live. Unless you are rich or well connected, the south east will have little to offer you. If there is a good river near you, simply head for the nearest large tackle shop and enquire about day tickets. Don't forget to buy a licence whilst you are there and take advice on which flies are most likely to be successful. Otherwise, choose a part of the country you have visited before and enjoyed and then look in the angling magazines for an angling hotel in that area. Get their brochure and check all the details before going any further. There is no point booking a week's angling holiday if you choose a week which is likely to be difficult or if there is no tuition or advice available. As a beginner, it is worth enquiring about the 'difficulty' of the water. You do not want to arrive at a hotel which has heavily wooded river banks with perilous slopes and difficult wading and the hotel won't want the responsibility and worry of a beginner either.

Once you get there, you will find that beats are allocated to guests on a rotating basis so that everyone has an opportunity to try the best stretches. Where to start on your beat should be no problem as hotel water is subject to intensive angling activity. You simply follow the paths and look for parts of the banking which are well trodden. As a beginner, it is probably best to choose a hotel water that is not exclusively dry fly as it is easier to start with wet fly. However the choice between wet and dry fly is not simple. Anglers not only disagree about the respective merits of both but they also indulge in heated debates about what constitutes an acceptable fly.

Wet or dry?

There is really nothing mysterious about angling with a fly. It is merely the throwing onto the water of an artificial representation of waterborne insects at various stages of their development. The artificial fly can be designed to copy the 'nymph' stage as it is coming loose from the weeds or stones in the river, the 'dun' which is moving up to the surface ready to hatch out or the 'spinner' which is the dying insect falling back onto the water after completing its mating dance. The idea is to get the imitation at the appropriate level of the water at the same time as the insect is developing and being eaten by the trout. Thus, nymphs and duns are fished under the water surface i.e. wet, and spinners are fished on the surface i.e. dry. Quite simple.

Trout also feed on other creatures in the water (grubs, molluscs etc.) and on the water (land-born insects which have dropped from trees or been blown down by the wind). As water-borne insects do not hatch out continuously throughout the day - they have the rather annoying habit of emerging at breakfast, lunch and teatime - it is handy for anglers to have the other life forms to imitate. This means that a fly can consist of anything from minute spinners to the garish lures mentioned earlier. It seems eminently sensible to me for anglers to try to imitate whatever is most likely to be eaten at the time you are on the river but you would not believe the furore such a notion creates in the angling world. Many male anglers not only despise but thoroughly abhor anything which is not a 'proper' fly and they enter into heated debates in the letters columns of angling magazines. The logic of these debates tends to be somewhat undermined by anglers' inability to agree on what a fly actually is in the first place and their purist aspirations. Joan Clarkson describes her 'benevolent uncle' tying a fly for the capture of a monster cannibal trout:

'The Benevolent Uncle finished what he was doing and held

the resulting object up to the light, examining it through half closed eyes. "No," he said after a moment. "No; it does not look like a Hairy Caterpillar."

"Is it meant to?" I asked innocently.

"Good God, no!" replied the Benevolent Uncle, hastily sticking the thing into his fly box.

I realised that I had been guilty of another error of taste and refrained from further enquiry, making a mental note that hairy caterpillars were in the same category as worms - not things to be mentioned in polite society.'

Needless to say, the Benevolent Uncle catches a monster with the fly which he then names Maxima Culpa!

Anglers also get quite miffy about the distinctions between wet and dry. Not only are the two flies fished at different levels of the water but the wet fly is cast across and downstream at roughly forty five degrees and then slowly retrieved. The dry fly is cast upstream with the line regathered at a speed which ensures that the fly travels along the water at the natural speed of the water so that it does not drag and create a wake behind it. In fast water and a strong wind this is quite difficult.

It seems reasonable to me to use either method, depending on the stage of development that the insect hatch has reached but, here again, powerful feelings come into play as it is generally considered that dry fly angling is the preferred method; the highest form of the art. This view is especially held by dry fly anglers with access to excellent water with good fly hatches.

As mentioned earlier, there is a good deal of snobbery about the virtues of fly versus bait angling for salmon but this has been elevated to ridiculous lengths on trout water. Whilst casting a fly is the most active, elegant and most satisfying way of catching a fish; and positioning a dry fly delicately in, front of a waiting trout in clear water and lifting to the take is indubitably a fine skill, I cannot for the life of me see why so many dry fly purists so deeply despise wet fly anglers. It is not as though the dry fly purists are content to get on with it, smirking with silent satisfaction at their assumed superiority. They are usually quite rude to other anglers and make derogatory statements to their faces. As anglers are mostly helpful, modest, polite people, I find this little aberration of theirs quite incomprehensible.

I think it is silly to restrict oneself to one method of trout angling. But, then so do the dry fly purists who are often to be seen casting a nymph (a 'wet' fly) upstream. Apparently this doesn't count as wet fly because the fly is still cast upstream! Maurice Wiggan in his excellent 'teach yourself' book, argues that it is only really sensible to dry fly on chalk streams and that everyone used wet flies originally. Much earlier, Charles Cotton recommended that you throw your fly according to the direction of the wind. This seems an excellent piece of advice to me.

In case you are wondering why I am making such a big issue about this business of wet or dry, upstream or down, I must stress that you need to know so that you will not unwittingly cause grave offence. Some waters are dry fly only and many have pretensions in that direction. If you persist in adopting an eclectic approach in such company you will lose friends who will scorn you. Irrational, but true, as I found out to my cost.

My husband and I had been invited to spend a day on the Dove by a couple of lengthy, though occasional, acquaintance. Our hostess had only recently taken to angling and had not had much success. It was early in the season; a drab, dull day which promised rain. As we approached the river there was no sign of fly life. In response to an enquiry from my husband, our host informed us that it was not 'dry fly only' but members were 'expected' to use dry fly. We dutifully proceeded to present dry flies, becoming more desultory in our casting as it was evident that there was not a surface feeding fish to be seen. Our host disappeared upriver and we decided to explore downstream with our hostess.

The stretch consisted of tight bends with numerous fast

runs under a steep opposite bank. Less than a third of the water was accessible to upstream casting, wading was difficult and it looked like perfect wet fly water. We were sorely tempted by the sight of water which had been untouched by the 'purists' and proved weak in our resolution. Egged on by our hostess who expressed a strong desire to learn how to present a wet fly, we promptly agreed to teach her. She had three fish in ten minutes and we succumbed totally, taking the limit of five brace each before dusk. We sat on the bank waiting for our host to find us, a few qualms setting in despite our hostess' obvious delight. Our host appeared tired and fishless. He gave us supper but I think our hostess' insistence on his taking a photograph of the three of us with our booty proved the last straw of his politeness. We still get Christmas cards. But that's all. So, you have been warned. You may, therefore, elect to skip the next section.

Casting a wet fly

This is the easiest method of trout angling except in a strong upstream wind when it will produce so many wind knots that you will quickly despair. You simply attach a nylon cast of about three pounds breaking strain to the end of your line. The cast has a handy loop so this requires only a simple knot. You then thread the tapered end of the cast through the eye of the hook of your chosen fly, twist it around the nylon several times and then thread the end through the loop, pulling it tight. You can get casts with two short droppers along the length of it to which you can attach two more flies which will cover different levels of the water after each cast. This means that you increase your chances of connecting with a fish but, unfortunately, it also increases the chances of getting tangled up so is best avoided in the early days. If you do get tangled up, it is easiest to undo by taking all the flies off before starting to unravel the tangle.

You then choose a streamy bit of water and start at the top the run. Simply cast across and down, letting the current swing the fly round and keep your line taut. Trout usually take as the line swings at an angle of about forty five degrees but they sometimes follow the fly after it stops at the edge of the current so retrieve it slowly for a few feet before casting again. It is worth casting two or three times in each spot before moving a pace or two downstream. It is easiest to wade downstream with the assistance of a wading stick but, in the early days, settle for feeling comfortable. Wade only within your capacity and remember that if the water is almost up to the top of your waders, as you bend slightly to net a fish the water will trickle down the back of your legs. Horrible.

Don't worry if you can't cast as far across the stream as you would like. You can cheat to get a bit of extra length by casting absolutely squarely across the river with a slack line. As soon as the fly lands, 'mend' the line sharply to the right (like twining a skipping rope) and your fly will hold the line you wanted although there is some danger of losing a fish if one takes before the line straightens out. If your flies end up in the branches of a tree rather than on the water, try a little twitch to release them first. If they become really stuck, then turn your head away before pulling hard - they hurtle across at you when they finally become free.

Trout usually take a wet fly in a definite manner and move away from you so there are few dangers of being caught with a slack line - the greatest sin in angling. That is why anglers say 'tight lines' instead of wishing you 'good luck.' Should the fish merely tweak the fly, you can cast over it again but if you feel a definite pull then move on as you will have frightened it out of taking again. If you have a day when you get a lot of tweaks and pulls but don't actually land a fish, then it is usual to say that the fish were 'taking short.' This doesn't actually mean anything but in the angling world is considered an acceptable excuse for a blank day.

As a hatch develops, the trout begin to feed more on the surface and you are now faced with a choice. You can either cast to rising fish with your wet flies, you can even turn round and cast them upstream although this is quite difficult, or you can change to a dry fly.

I do not propose to go into the intricacies of dry fly as I do not consider myself sufficiently proficient to cast anything but a short upstream line. The complexities of the shepherd's crook and curved left casts remain a mystery to me. Also, there is an excellent account in Maurice Wiggan's book which clearly explains both simple and advanced casting techniques.

Wet and dry

I think the easiest thing for the beginner to do is to avoid the whole controversy of wet versus dry. Charles Cotton's advice on casting with the wind is sensible. I am able to follow it fully as most of my trout angling is done on the Eden, which flows from south to north, and the adjoining Eamont, which flows from west to east. As my next-door neighbour has a weather-vane on his roof, I can make a decision about the wind before I even set out from our holiday home. Although the wind is a major consideration, especially when it is what the weather forecasters euphemistically refer to as 'fresh,' I also tend to prefer a wet fly in the early part of the season, favouring a dry fly as the season progresses and the early summer sedges begin to start the fish feeding in the evening.

The main thing to do is to allow your timing with the rod to become relaxed and comfortable. Never flog on, thrashing the water when things are going badly. It is much better to retire to the bank, collect your composure and look around. In trout angling you are more on your own than in other branches of angling. This means that you are less observed and have more time to develop your own style and technique. Only time will tell whether you develop into the technical/handyman sort of angler or whether you become more of an artist. I suspect that you are more likely to become the latter because women's socialisation encourages a more patient and sensual approach to angling. As the expert, Geoffrey Bucknall has commented in *Salmon, Trout and Sea Trout* (November 1989):

'Some frenetic guys - casting machines really - keep pump-
ing out the fly, but I'm sure that the relaxed angler is the most
successful. This may explain why women are often the dead-
liest exponents of the art.'

Cooking trout

Unlike salmon and sea trout angling where you often have
more fish than you can eat immediately, a trout catch is likely
to be more modest in proportion and you can decide whether
to eat it for supper or not on the day of the catch. Select the
most beautiful specimen; gut and wash it, and then simply fry
it in a little butter. Add a squeeze of lemon juice and a
scattering of parsley to some fresh butter in the pan. Remember to open a bottle of wine and you will have the perfect
ending to a good day on the river which no amount of cream
or almonds can improve.

If it is not convenient to cook and eat your fish immediately,
give them to friends or freeze them to hand over to friends
later. You will not enhance your reputation as either cook or
angler if you regularly feed guests on the accumulated, as-
sorted trout in your freezer. Leave your friends to pour over
the recipe books for more involved ways of cooking trout and
they will enjoy it. You, of course, will realise how lucky you are
to have the privilege of selected, fresh-from-the-river, trout. If
you do need to show off, the following *Good Food Guide* recipe
from the Old House Hotel, Wickham, is excellent for fresh fish
but dead fiddly.

La Truite de Souvenir

4 fresh trout.
For the soufflé sauce: 1 oz butter, 1 tablesp flour, half pint milk,
2 eggs (separated) and 4 egg whites, 2-3 oz grated cheese, salt
and pepper, pinch of nutmeg, a little milk and seasoned flour,
2-3 oz butter.

Clean and bone the trout. It is not easy, so get your partner
to take the responsibility for this part. Filleting knives are

regularly advertised in the angling magazines and make this job easier. Prepare the soufflé first. Make a roux with the butter and flour, add the milk and stir until it thickens. Away from the heat, stir in the egg yolks, then the cheese, and season lightly. Wash the trout, dip them in milk, and then in seasoned flour. Melt the butter in a large pan and brown the trout in it, turning after about three minutes. Place in well buttered gratin dishes. Whisk the egg whites stiffly and gently fold the soufflé mixture into them. Cover the trout with this mixture and bake at regulo 6, 400°F or 200°C for 20 minutes until the soufflé is light golden brown. Serve immediately.

If you are fortunate enough to catch lots of trout of equal quality and size, you might like to try smoking them. Home smokers are simple to use but unless you are particularly fond of smoked trout it is an expensive way to make smoked trout paté. It can also be rather bland and I think a mixture of trout and eel is better.

Trout and Eel Paté (a Pool Court recipe)
2 smoked trout, a quarter lb smoked eel, fresh chives, 3 fluid oz double cream, salt and pepper.
For the béchamel: half an oz butter and flour, 6 fluid oz milk, 3 eggs, 2 oz butter.
Make the bechamel using the butter, flour, milk and seasoning. Allow it to cool slightly before whisking in egg yolks and butter. Skin and flake the trout carefully with a fork and chop the eel finely. Fold into the sauce with the chives when it is cool. Stiffly beat the double cream and then the egg whites. Fold first one, then the other, into the fish mixture. Refrigerate thirty minutes before serving as it is quite soft and creamy.

CHAPTER FIVE

GRAYLING ANGLING

A funny sort of fish

In river board classification terms, the grayling *(thymallus thymallus)* is considered to be a coarse fish. It has a mouth developed for bottom feeding and, unlike salmon, trout and sea trout, it spawns between March and May which means that you cannot catch it during this period. However, it is technically a game fish because it has an adipose fin like other members of the salmon family. No one is quite sure where it originates from and how it came to inhabit British rivers. All writers agree that it is an Ice Age fish, with some thinking that it naturalised in the country around that time, whilst others subscribe to an importation-by-monks theory.

Certainly, it has been present in Scotland and parts of northern England for centuries but became actively stocked in rivers only when angling became increasingly popular in the second half of the nineteenth century. The main motivation was to lengthen the angling season by two or three months because of the graylings' different spawning season. I am not sure about the naturalisation theory as they were definitely introduced artificially into the Eden and Eamont which are both north enough to have been included in the area consid-ered natural for the fish. Unusually, there is an eye witness account of this event:

'The life history of the grayling in the Eden is comparatively short. They were put in as 'fry' at Musgrave about the year 1880. I had an uncle living there then, and he had a good deal to do with it, although he protested to his friend, who was at the bottom of the business, that the river carried its full head of trout and any competitor in regard to the food supply would be injurious.' (Nelson, 1922)

Whilst the grayling can be considered a game fish, it does not look even remotely like any other members of the salmon family. To my eyes it is a rather drab, smallish fish of greyish colour with a lot of coarse scales. I find it most unrecognisable from accounts in angling books, where it is usually the subject of glowing descriptions such as 'its skin is shot with colours like a piece of oiled silk' and 'a fish from the Ice Age . . . its silver sides tinged with mauve, and its great dorsal fin like a banner.' This fin is likened to the sail of a yacht and the fish is always referred to in female terms - usually on the lines of 'silver lady' or 'princess of the stream.' This is rather odd in itself as all other game fish are always referred to as 'he.' For example, Hugh Falkus in his book on sea trout says:

. . . the grayling . . . is always a 'she'.

85

'Henceforth to avoid confusion in grammatical construction, a fish is frequently referred to by the masculine pronoun rather than the more usual neuter pronoun 'it.' I am aware of the irony involved, since in a season's catch my females outnumber males by at least 2:1. Early in the season the proportion is more like 20:1. Nevertheless, for the sake of clarity they are all masculine here.'

So, other game fish are male even when they are mostly female yet the grayling (which is probably fairly equal in proportion of males to females), is always a 'she.' This in itself is enough to make one smell a rat. Obviously there is some sort of deliberate hype surrounding the grayling.

Whilst I openly admit that the grayling I have encountered have been out of season and therefore out of condition, I still can't connect with any of these rhapsodic accounts and I am intrigued by the contrived passion it arouses in anglers. No-one seems neutral about grayling. They are either strongly pro- or anti- grayling. The pro-school not only wax eloquent about its physical perfections but they also maintain that it takes more skill to catch grayling than other game fish. The famous angler, Charles Ritz, maintains that only real fishermen appreciate its true worth. Lawrence Koller argues that netting and removing it from trout water, which many anglers do, 'must take really a hobnailed prejudice to treat a fish like the grayling thus.'

Grayling detractors draw attention to the fact that it is not a discerning fish and will take any fly which has a bright colour or bit of tinsel about it. They also consider it vermin and worry about it taking feed from trout. Grayling do inhabit similar sorts of water as trout and do feed on insects - the powerful dorsal fin, large air bladder, and long sight of the fish enable it to rise almost vertically from the river bottom to the water surface to take a fly. However, they prefer fast flowing water over muddy bottoms where they shoal and feed at all levels as opposed to trout which prefer fast flowing water with stony or gravel bottoms.

Willcock is a lone voice of sanity in the debate about the relative merits of grayling. He describes it as a betwixt-and-between fish: which it plainly is. He argues that few anglers fish for grayling specifically, using it more as a stopgap during the trout closed season and that this gives anglers an inescapable feeling that 'we are slumming in the piscatorial sense.' I think there is a lot in this. Whatever its proponents say, it does not fight like other game fish, it doesn't look like them, and it is barely edible.

The only grayling I have caught have been accidents whilst trout angling. I can always tell when I have hooked a grayling because you get the sensation of having a heavy weight on the end of the line due to the grayling putting up its large dorsal fin which acts like a kind of drogue. You slowly but firmly pull it in and then make the mistake that I did with my first grayling. I handled it to get the hook out gently before returning it to the river. Don't believe all this stuff about grayling smelling slightly of thyme when freshly caught. They stink.

. . . . remove the hook without touching the fish . . .

And your hand will continue to stink for ages. Nowadays I try to remove the hook without touching the fish at all.

As I said earlier in this book, I can't see any rationale for catching fish which I can't then eat. And proof that the grayling is inedible comes from the anglers who say they eat them. They caution one to scrape off the scales carefully and admit that the flesh is rather 'coarse.' As they are easily reared, they would be extensively fish farmed if they were really edible. I think that the main reason why the grayling continues to be eulogised about has little to do with the small number of grayling anglers' pride and pleasure and a lot to do with angling magazines' shortage of 'live' material for the winter editions. Come late autumn and the grayling will make its regular appearance on the printed page, with its predictably over the top prose.

Should you actually find yourself sufficiently tempted by the prospect of grayling angling in the middle of winter, then I suggest that you read Charles Ritz' book - *A Fly Fisher's Life* - in which he gives the most exact details of how to set about it. Myself, I shall occupy the close season with memories of the past season and hopes of the one to come, my mind firmly focussed on salmon, brown trout and sea trout.

CHAPTER SIX

SEA TROUT ANGLING

A new experience

Sea trout are similar to salmon and brown trout in many respects but are a totally different experience when you feel one on the end of your line. No other game fish fights quite like a sea trout. From the moment it is hooked it is in continuous movement. It leaps out of the water astonishingly high before crashing back down and making more tremendous runs. Most game fish attempt to run away from the angler when hooked but sea trout have a disconcerting habit of racing towards the angler at a faster speed than the loose line this creates can be wound onto the reel. Before you have time to collect your senses or your line, it puts in a series of spectacular leaps and then charges off again. Even a small sea trout gives an angler a truly heart stopping experience. An acquaintance of ours who hooked a large sea trout in the dark of night, said that he was alarmed to hear the heavy thudding sounds of someone on the bank. It was some moments before he realised that he was listening anxiously to the pounding of his heart.

Rarely does an angler feel truly in control when playing a sea trout, and the fish's fighting qualities is one of the main reasons that although it is a betwixt and between fish in some respects, as the grayling is, sea trout angling engenders a vast snob value whilst the grayling is always second best. The successful sea trout angler is highly regarded amongst the angling fraternity. Another reason why sea trout are prized so highly is the extreme shyness of the fish. It is said to have excellent eyesight and be extremely sensitive to vibrations, making it not only instantly wary of the clumsy angler's movements but likely to spread panic through an entire shoal, causing them to bolt to another pool. Thus, stealth and casting a long line are usually advised for sea trout angling: characteristics which will mark the sea trout angler as a very superior sort of practitioner.

So, quite what sort of fish is this highly prized specimen which has a greater snob value than salmon even though it rarely equals the salmon in size? It was originally thought to be a distinct species of trout but it is now generally agreed that it is a brown trout which has adopted a migratory habit. It spends the first three years of its life in the river before becoming a smolt in much the same way as a salmon, lingering in the estuary feeding on sand eels and shrimps, and then going out to sea for more intensive feeding. Often it returns to the river of birth after only a few months at sea. At this stage, it is returning with larger, older fish but, unlike them, it will not necessarily spawn. It is almost as though it has come along for the trip. These shoals of differing sized sea trout then return to the sea. They do not suffer the same mortality as salmon after the run in the river and frequently make several trips to sea and river. This means that a sea trout can be of any weight from under a pound to a top weight of around twenty pounds and any age from four to twelve years. Sea trout have different names in different parts of the country, particularly the smaller ones which are known as sewin, peal, white trout and so on. My favourite name for smaller, younger sea trout is the South West Irish one, where they are called juniors.

Despite the capacity for sea trout to reach large weights, any fish over six pounds is considered to be a specimen fish and well worth boasting about. Sea trout return to the river mainly in the summer in shoals, running in shorter bursts and lower water than salmon although the bigger fish often run early and alone. A large sea trout can look remarkably like a salmon except that its head resembles a brown trout and it has a squared tail end unlike the forked salmon tail. Neither does it have a 'wrist' at the base of its tail like a salmon as you will find out if you try to 'hand tail' it like a salmon; at which point it will simply slip out of your grip. Even if you are not sure that you have a large sea trout on the end of your line by the way it fights, you will soon find out when you try to net it. Whilst a tired salmon will fold into quite a small net, a sea trout remains rigid and cannot be netted until it is completely played out. It can then be eased into a net which is large enough to encompass the entire length of the fish. The slightest knock of the net rim on the fish and the hook will come out and the fish will be back in the water. As I found out the hard way.

Smaller sea trout resemble brown trout closely although they are much more silvery. They are said to be indistinguishable from brown trout in early life but I always think they look different. As a smolt, the sea trout is distinguished from a salmon smolt by its adipose fin which remains orange. No-one knows why some brown trout become sea going but a similar thing happens in North America where rainbow trout become migratory steelheads in some rivers. Bernard Venables proposes the theory that rivers with rich feeding have brown trout whilst those with poorer feeding have sea trout.

There is some logic in this theory although no real certainty. For example, the Torridge, which has salmon, sea trout and brown trout, rarely yields native brown trout of more than nine inches long. The Eden also has all species with excellent brown trout but these are to be found in the upper reaches and the sea trout rarely run far up the river. Generally, sea trout spawn much lower down a river than salmon. However, there are some notable exceptions to this pattern. Many Scottish rivers with poor food supplies are teeming with small brown trout but no sea trout and the Tweed has salmon, sea trout and brown trout - all of excellent size.

So, really, sea trout are a bit of a mystery; belonging to the brown trout family but having many of the habits of salmon.

They are betwixt and between in their feeding habits also. Whilst brown trout feed on fly life in the river and salmon feed in the sea, sea trout seem to do a bit of both. Hugh Falkus maintains that only non-spawning sea trout feed in fresh water and he substantiates his argument by quoting statistics which have shown that only 20% of sea trout examined in rich feeding waters of Ireland had anything in their stomachs. He bolsters his argument by pointing out that the methods used to catch sea trout suggest that they do not feed much in fresh water. You don't have to be an entomologist to hook sea trout in Britain. Most of the flies used do not represent real insects, being bushy, brightly coloured creatures. Lures are also used and I have seen a small sea trout with an even smaller fish in its mouth after capture so I think it is probably accurate to assume that only the smaller sea trout do feed in fresh water in Britain.

However, Ireland is a different matter altogether. I have frequently seen sea trout taking daddy long legs on Lough Currane in Co Kerry and 'dapping' with these insects - dancing them gently on the water surface - is a popular method of sea trout angling in Ireland. Falkus would maintain that these are just the small, non-spawning fish, and that they only seem big because their eyesight makes them clumsy in their attempts to grab insects, causing them to make a large wake in the water as they miss as many insects as they take. This seems a rather odd conclusion in view of all that it said about their keen eyesight and extreme caution, which is supposed to be such that they are easily frightened by the shape of a boat, and require a long, delicate cast to get near them.

It is an even odder conclusion for me as I have hooked sea trout so near the boat on Lough Currane that a strike once lifted the fish out of the water and over the boat. I found my scepticism about large sea trout not feeding in fresh water further strengthened yet again on Lough Currane. It was a hot, still day and we had lingered over lunch, waiting for the wind to get up. In all fairness I must point out that we lingered for other reasons as well - my husband and boatman, Vincent O'Sullivan, were engrossed in opening and eating huge crabs which Vincent had removed from his lobster pots that morning. They were somewhat hampered by the limits of their equipment - one blunt knife and a pair of angling forceps. The lake remained flat calm and glassy and we sat in the boat contentedly looking at the scenery. Suddenly rings of feeding fish began to appear and we watched fascinated as the activity intensified. The fish were feeding on red ants and there were hundreds of fish, of all sizes, around us. Our fascination turned to frustration as the wind failed to appear - the feast tantalisingly slowed and then petered out before a gentle breeze finally rose.

So, no-one can convince me that sea trout of all sizes and ages do not feed at some time in fresh water although I would agree with the general opinion that they soon lose the feeding habit as they get near to spawning time. On Lough Currane sea trout are usually taken in the main body of the lake and although they can be seen splashing around in the water lilies at the river mouths, they rarely take there - unlike the salmon of the lake.

The unpredictability of sea trout feeding and their tendency to run to the spawning grounds in shorter more persistent bursts than salmon has given them an added mystery for the angler. Myths about their being particularly capricious and temperamental abound.

Myths about sea trout angling

It has become almost *de rigeur* for sea trout anglers to practise their art at the dead of night. This obviously deters a lot of men and is a serious drawback for women anglers. Even if you do not mind stumbling over a field full of cows on your way to the river bank, climbing unsighted over barbed-wire fences and hoping that the eery hooting howl you can hear is in fact an owl and not a werewolf, is it safe for women to go out alone at night? If you survive the actual angling, will the car journey be without risk? It looks as though sea trout angling is out for women. But is this night time stuff quite as essential as is made out?

This notion of sea trout as shy, finicky creatures of the night has built up over many years. For example, Gray comments about the Torridge:

'The taking time (for salmon) is usually only about half an hour at early dusk and with a strong trout rod you ought to be able to manage two at least, and three if you are quick, before it gets too dark for salmon and you turn your attention to peal.'

The final stamp of approval on night angling was given with the publication of Hugh Falkus' book on the subject; a book which is widely regarded by male anglers as definitive. The book is confidently entitled *Sea Trout Fishing: A Guide to Success* and is based on the author's success at sea trout angling on the border Esk and his careful study of sea trout behaviour in this crystal clear river. The river is ideal for detailed observation and Falkus has made it his life study.

His knowledge and prowess on the Esk are beyond doubt, but I think he should have been more wary of generalising from one river, and more aware of his own particular angling philosophy, as he is in danger of misleading and discouraging the beginner. So sure is he that sea trout rarely feed in fresh water, that they are shy, capricious creatures which move at night, that he pushes the case for night-time angling beyond my reach. He elevates night angling to a level where he makes it obvious that this is an activity for the 'real' man. For example, he states emphatically:

'Sea trout will take the lure at any time during hours of darkness, providing the night is dark enough. As a result, the most likely period is usually between one and three o'clock in the morning. Small wonder that I view with pity the fisherman who packs up at midnight.' And 'Bright moonlight is not suitable . . . darkness is the important factor.' And 'Nothing I have written is intended to imply that night fishing is easy . . .

But of course, night fishing is not to everyone's taste; not every fisherman is temperamentally suited to the sport. Like wild-fowling, it has a strong, rather weird mystique, an appreciation of which demands an affinity with solitude in wild and remote places. Anyone who does not derive a deep delight from long hours in the darkness by some lonely river, with only the wind and water as his companions should abandon any thoughts of serious night fishing.' And 'To a small but devoted band of anglers, however, sea trout night fishing represents the very cream of sport.'

Well, that alone should be enough to deter the average woman of somewhat craven disposition. Especially one such as myself who balks at the idea of coming face to face with a bullock in the day time never mind the horrors of picking my way through a field which might be full of them gently sleeping until I trip over one by accident. However, there is even more to discourage women. He reckons that allowing our minds to become one with the surroundings - something I always regard

. . . is it safe for women to go out alone at night?

as peaceful harmony - is actually an intuitive faculty which is part of man's hunting instinct, an atavistic survival trait. Oh dear. One consolation is that it rarely does ever get really dark on northern rivers in the summer months.

And there is even more in store. His book is highly technical; full of diagrams instructing one how to splice, tie complicated knots, judge the hook angle etc, which I find difficult to follow. There are photographs too. Even one of a cowpat, under which we are assured that we can always find worms should we need them. I studied the 22 photograph sequence depicting every stage of the steeple cast, without which apparently no-one can be assured of success in sea trout angling, with complete bewilderment!

The message comes across loud and clear. Sea trout angling is for the technically proficient, highly skilled man who readily endures complete solitude and pitch darkness. Thank goodness I didn't read it until after I had already caught quite a few sea trout in daylight in both England and Ireland. Also, I had already enjoyed the wonderful sight of sea trout jumping up a fish pass on the river Inny on a gloriously hot summer's afternoon. I am delighted to report that this pitch black, night time angling and shy sea trout business is an elaborate male myth. It is one way to catch sea trout but it is not the only way. Jean Green, an angler on the Wear, averages four large sea trout (5-12 lbs) each year in daylight.

Day time sea trout angling

River angling for sea trout can involve spinning, worming or artificial flies - all the methods used to catch salmon and brown trout. So the methods are sufficiently similar to be familiar but the techniques needed are significantly different. This is borne out by the fact that catching a sea trout by accident when angling for salmon or brown trout is not a common occurrence. You can't really cast a bait or fly into the water which is abundant in all three types of fish and hope to have an equal chance of catching any of them. You actually have to make up your mind to go for sea trout and adapt your technique accordingly.

The techniques used for salmon angling are generally too slow to attract sea trout except south west Irish rivers where both move readily to a fly presented quickly and high in the water. I always speed up for sea trout (I am not referring to worming here as I haven't yet tried this method with sea trout). For sea trout spinning you need a small spinner and a quick retrieve. On rivers where spinning is allowed, I have found that a small silver spoon, cast upstream and across and then wound quickly back, is effective.

Using this technique I once took three fish in quick succession from a single pool. The first was about three quarters of a pound, the next around a pound and a half and the third a good two pounds. I did hook a larger one immediately after but lost this through sloppy netting. Sea trout are said to lie in shoals roughly in order of size, with the largest at the front of the shoal and I must say that the weight sequence of my three fish seemed to confirm this.

What is of more interest to the beginning woman sea trout angler is that I caught them all in broad daylight, in the middle of the afternoon, in low water and in the confines of a narrow stream. So much for the sea trout are timid creatures with good eyesight notion. All my limited success with sea trout in English rivers has been when I have been covering the middle section of a stream's run, a little higher up than one would expect good brown trout to be lying and a little lower down than salmon which tend to lie in the neck of pools as the season gets under way.

The technique for fly angling is similar to that used for brown trout but Jean Green recommends a thirteen and a half foot rod or longer so that a pool can be fished without undue wading or false casting. She avoids handlining as much as possible but keeps the fly moving in slower water by 'mending' her line downstream after the cast. She always uses a single fly and keeps a loop of line in her hand to release as soon as a fish takes. The flies which attract sea trout in rivers are bigger and brighter than those for brown trout and you can cast them upstream or down. Popular flies are mallard and claret, Peter Ross, teal and silver, blue charm and the Zulu. They are all effective but local advice is always worth having.

The trouble with sea trout angling is that only too often a fish seems well hooked but then suddenly the hook comes out for no apparent good reason. This happens more in the early part of the season and is said to happen because sea trout have soft mouths when they enter the river. I am not sure whether this is true or not as the fly doesn't seem to tear out, rather it just drops out. I have not investigated sea trout mouths too closely because, like brown trout and salmon, they have extremely sharp teeth and one cut across the nail bed of a forefinger was enough to make me wary. Whatever the reason for sea trout losing the fly, it is most frustrating.

Often sea trout 'offer' at a fly and you feel a sort of double pluck and then nothing. Pudepha gives some excellent advice for this situation. He recommends that you give the fish time to return to its lie by counting sixty seconds before recasting. This also gives you time to calm down from the excitement and make a rather better cast than you might otherwise do.

The best thing to do in sea trout angling is to always hope, fervently. This seems to work as well as anything, especially when you are playing a fish which is charging madly around, putting in acrobatic leaps and generally giving you a feeling of intense excitement mingled with complete ineptitude. One school of thought advises you to drop your rod point when the fish jumps so that the line tension won't be overstrained when the fish lands back in the water. Another school advises you to hold the rod even higher. I don't think it matters very much unless you have superb reflexes and are quick witted as mostly you will be too spellbound to do either thing. It is a useful piece of advice though if you are watching someone playing a sea trout. I was sheltering under a tree in heavy rain when my husband hooked a large and energetic sea trout of about four pounds. After making several charges up and down stream, it suddenly shot straight towards my husband. Literally inches away from his feet, it leapt six feet in the air, twisted round and thrashed back into the water, shedding the hook in the process. My husband was too taken aback to do anything, even to me when I commented sweetly 'shouldn't you have dropped your rod tip, darling?'

Sea trout angling on lakes is quite a different matter altogether. The most important thing here is to hire a good boatman as the positioning of the boat on the correct drift will make all the difference. Drifting a boat sounds quite simple. All you do is put the boat sideways onto the wind, sit astride the seat and begin casting as the boat gently drifts with the wind. However, the boat has to be maintained on the drift by means of judicious use of one oar at the back of the boat and considerable athleticism is required as the boat reaches the end of the drift and a rocky shore looms in front of you. There are numerous accounts in the angling literature of lone men who hook gigantic sea trout at this very moment, holding the rod in their teeth whilst they manoeuvre the boat away from

. . . my teeth would be unequal to the situation.

the rocks in a force ten gale. Well, fine for them. Myself, I prefer an experienced boatman on these occasions. It is not only my teeth which would be unequal to the situation.

The beauty of lake angling for sea trout on the drift is that the wind is behind you so you are always warm and dry. Even in the strongest wind or heaviest downpour, all you need to do is pull your hood up and you are secure from the elements - until you hook a fish and have to play it behind the boat, that is. Unless you are dapping with daddy long legs, you need a sea trout rod of about eleven feet for this type of angling, a strong enough cast to cope with a big fish, and a team of three flies. Your boatman will advise you, but generally traditional sea trout flies are used in Britain whilst in Ireland you will need flies which are more representative of the real insects around, particularly those which come off the heather. Popular flies in Ireland are the Connemara black, Green Peter, soldier palmer, fiery brown, Bibio, and golden olive. My own particular favourite is a very pretty fly called a claret bumble. They are not cheap and it is worth getting a good selection from a reputable stockist before setting off to Ireland as you don't want to find yourself with one that comes to pieces once it has been in a single sea trout mouth. As you start each drift, you simply pull out some line and cast it in front of you. This is fairly easy as the wind is behind and assisting you. Do, however, remember that there are other people in the boat with you and cast carefully so that you don't all get tangled up together. Once the flies land on the water, you need to retrieve them immediately as the boat is drifting onto them, causing your line to go slack unless you remember to smoothly cast, retrieve, recast. Despite what most of the experts say, I have not found it necessary to cast a long line. Indeed, most sea trout seem to take almost at the point of lift off before recasting. Sometimes they leave the take so late that your flies are already in the air for the next cast and all you see is the swirl of the fish. If this happens, quickly recast a very short line and hope that the fish comes at the flies again.

When the fish shows, strike immediately. This is where the longer sea trout rod is useful as you often need the extra length to make the strike - almost backwards over your shoulder when the fish takes near the boat. So that other people in the boat don't have to stop angling every time you hook a fish, you are supposed to get the fish under control quickly and then bring it round the other side of the boat where you play it out until it is ready for netting. This is not too difficult with juniors but the larger sea trout often have different ideas. It is most disconcerting to have swung your legs round the seat, often wrapping yards of line round your feet in the process, and then find that the fish has decided to run deep under the boat or, even worse, across the lines of the other anglers. I am assured that if a sea trout remains under the boat it is possible to pass the rod under too but I haven't had to attempt this yet. When the fish dashes under other anglers' lines, you soon find out who your friends are and whether you are capable of following Charles Cotton's admirable dictum: *

'Be so ever provided as to be able to help yourself in all exigencies; nor deem it a small incivility to interrupt your companion in his sport.'

Anyway, it is the most tremendous fun. There are just one or two snags about which it is as well to be forewarned. However long a particular drift may be, never stop retrieving to blow your nose or think your own thoughts. The boat will drift only too quickly onto your line, especially if the wind is anything more than the slightest zephyr, and your flies will get hooked on the bottom of the boot. This is to be avoided as it will involve you in leaning perilously over the edge of the boat with a length of stick, vainly prodding about to loosen the flies. If you do need to stop for a moment, begin the cast but do not propel it forwards allowing the line to fall onto the water behind you. Here your flies will safely trail away from the boat. Sometimes you hook a fish whilst your flies are in this position. In Ireland, this is called 'mousetrapping.'

On a long drift, the constant casting and retrieving can

become a bit repetitive and lull you into a calm sort of monotony when there isn't much action. Most anglers advise a slight change in the speed of the retrieve in this situation but my husband maintains that it is therapeutic and soothing. I tend to concentrate more and try hardest when the wind is in the south or west, especially if it is a bit rainy as these conditions seem the best.

The only other snags with angling from a boat on a lake depend upon the delicacy or otherwise of your complexion and constitution. The sun reflects from the water even on dullish days and there is always a danger of sun or wind burn. Most people remember to put protective cream on their noses and wear tinted glasses but large parts of your neck also get exposed so it is worth applying a liberal coating of cream all over your neck. Also, the swell on a large lake can be quite heavy in a strong wind so if you have the slightest tendency to sea sickness, it is worth taking medication before you set out.

I am surprised that all the myths about sea trout angling and machismo are to do with rivers and not lakes because I think that sea trout angling from a boat is actually the most physically arduous of all the angling I do. The constant casting is demanding, especially as a long and single handed rod is used. I have seen some exhausted looking men in the bar at the end of a long day on the lake but they don't seem to make a big issue about this.

As long as you remember to take a good selection of rods with you, preferably your older ones, you can always take to trolling if you get tired of fly angling on a big lake. This involves positioning spinning rods at right angles from the sides of the boat and trailing the spinners on about thirty yards of line as your boatman motors along the lake. You don't actually do much apart from sit quietly whilst this is going on as the boatman is the vital person and you aren't even needed to strike if you put a stone on your line to indicate a take. Mind you, when a fish takes, it is all hands to the mill, as one person must play the fish and the others must hurriedly wind in the other lines. There is a special concentration and skill needed for this type of angling which I don't have. I tend to look around at the scenery instead of focussing on the lines and I soon get cold and bored. Still, it is exciting in small doses.

Cooking sea trout

The main thing to remember when cooking sea trout is that it is a trout - even though it may be the size and colour of a salmon. If you have a large one, it can be cooked like salmon although Conrad Voss Bark's method is the simplest - he puts butter, salt, pepper and a sprinkle of dry sherry in the fish's stomach, wraps it in a couple of damp sheets of a tabloid newspaper and places it in the oven. When the paper is bone dry and burnt at the edges it is not only ready but the skin comes away with the paper. However, your guests may be disappointed that it does not taste like salmon. Juniors are easy as you just treat them like brown trout. Bigger ones pose a little bit of a problem.

Unless you particularly like the delicate flavour, I think they are better for the addition of some vegetables to the cooking liquid and accompanied by a sauce such as Hollandaise. The following recipe is reliable - yet another Pool Court recipe. I include their instructions for Hollandaise sauce too.

Baked Sea Trout

4 trout fillets, 3 oz unsalted butter, 2 tablesp mixed herbs such as parsley, chervil, chives and dill, juice of 1 lemon, 1 small leek, 2 medium carrots, 2 sticks celery, 2 fluid oz white wine, seasoning.

Wash and trim the vegetables and peel the carrots. Cut into very thin strips, the size of matchsticks. Blend 2 oz of the butter with the herbs and lemon juice. Cut four large oblongs of aluminium foil and lightly butter. Divide the vegetables into four and place in the middle of the foil. Cover with a trout fillet. Top with a nob of the herb butter. Bring up the sides of the foil, season the fish and add a tablespoon of wine. Close the parcel and bake on a tray at 200°C, 400°F or regulo 6-7 for 15-20 minutes. Open carefully and serve with Hollandaise sauce.

Hollandaise sauce

3 tablesp cold water, 1 teasp crushed white peppercorns, 1 tablesp white wine vinegar, 3 egg yolks, 9 oz melted unsalted butter, juice half lemon.

Mix together in a pan the peppercorns, vinegar and 2 tablesp of the cold water. Reduce by half over a moderate heat. Remove from the heat. Put the egg yolks and 1 tablesp of cold water in a glass bowl. Whisk lightly and add sieved reduction a little at a time, stirring well. Place the bowl over a pan of gently simmering water and whisk continuously until thick and creamy (don't allow it to get too hot). Whisk in the butter a little at a time. If it becomes too thick, add a little lukewarm water. Season and add a few drops of lemon juice. Serve immediately.

Hints on how to avoid this sauce 'cracking' can be found in *Recipe Secrets* by Michael Gill.

CHAPTER SEVEN

EXTRA INFORMATION

Contemplation

Anglers are often heard saying silly things - like not minding if they don't catch fish. This is certainly an odd statement to hear from a group of people who entertain a consuming passion for catching fish. It is the basest of lies but it does also have an element of truth in it. What it means is that there is more to angling than just catching fish. The context is important and anglers often try to convey this on paper with the floweriest of descriptions about the wonders of nature.

These descriptions are utterly boring to anyone but anglers and the ordinary reader could be forgiven for assuming that an appreciation of nature is the 'other half' of angling. If this were the case, anglers arriving at a river for a week's holiday and finding the river in flood, dirty and unfishable, would happily settle for a naturalist walk on the river bank. Closer examination of the thwarted angler shows that this is not the case at all.

The frustrated angler tries unsuccessfully to enjoy a lingering breakfast but the food tastes like ash and lies heavy in the stomach. After unseeingly munching as many pieces of toast as possible, the angler is finally driven out of the hotel by the stern glances of the waitresses who are by now setting the tables for the next meal and a visit to look at the water takes place. The angler knows that the water can't possibly have dropped at all as the rain still drives onto the window panes but perversely hopes a miracle has taken place during breakfast. The water is inspected and little sticks poked hopefully onto the bank to mark the rise or fall of the water. It is still brown and banktop.

Does the angler turn away from the dirty water and enjoy the miracles of nature? Not at all. A visit to the tackle shop enables the angler's thoughts to remain on fish and things fishy. But this only fills in the time until about eleven o'clock, even if the most extravagant purchases are indulged. The time until lunch must be filled up somehow. Does the angler now set his or her mind to the beauties of nature? Again, not at all. A bit of aimless shopping usually follows while the local inhabitants view with amusement the sad sight of anxious anglers mooching miserably around, their four-wheel drive cars cluttering up the car parks like swans blown off the river into the fields. Lengthy lunches reverberate with the sounds of loud hollow laughter and then the river is inspected again.

The little sticks indicate that the water has dropped an inch or two and the anglers, quicker than the more sensible river birds, return making excited sounds of delight and anticipation as they feel the water around their feet, sniffing the air in anticipation. They are suddenly completely engrossed and re-interested in the wildlife around them; 'did you see that dipper?' 'Oh, look at those marigolds.' Something takes place between the actual catching of fish and the appreciation of nature which is impossible to describe. It involves the process, as much as the practice, of angling and most of us explain it as the contemplative side of angling - the utter balm of the mind.

Indubitably, it is the contemplative nature of angling which sets it apart from field sports but it is difficult to portray until you actually experience it. It is rather more than a simple rest of the brain, much more than the quiet rumination of a sheep and rather less than a total communing with nature and the thinking of philosophical thoughts. Your mind is still on catching fish however much you appreciate the wildlife, the peacefulness or the profundity of it all.

The notion of quiet, peaceful contemplation whilst angling is probably nothing more than the results of the state of mind necessary to catch fish. If you are concentrating wholeheartedly on catching fish then your mind cannot be concentrating on anything else. For me, this means that I am not thinking about domestic or work issues and neither am I entertaining a single evil thought. And very pleasant it is too. Unfortunately, the philosophy behind the art has become elevated in popular angling mythology. It has become *de rigeur* only to go angling in total peace and solitude, far from the madding crowd. Certainly far from the madding family. You can't concentrate on fish with the kids around.

This means that angling is largely viewed as something which men do, preferably miles away from the nearest human habitation. Now it may well be true that angling at its purest can only be practised on a remote hill loch, reached after a three mile trek over difficult terrain but I think this reflects male notions about privacy rather than female ones. For many years now, my notions regarding privacy in the home have been simple ones concerning mainly whether or not there is a lock on the bathroom door. Similarly, privacy and contemplation of the river are equally small scale. And I enjoy other people being around when I catch fish.

Contented contemplation in angling does not necessitate a hard, rough slog to remote and isolated waters any more than success in catching is dictated by advanced technical proficiency. These are just macho ideas about angling, more to do with a sense of what a proper male angler should be like than in reality. However, this myth of the 'proper' lone angler is prevalent in the literature and the stereotype can be off-putting for women who can't set off to remote locations on their own. And it means that there is an etiquette which is not explained, a lot of things don't get said and you are left wondering what to do if you fall in, how to behave in a boat, what ghillies will expect and so on.

This is a disadvantage to male anglers too. If they feel

obliged to be perfectly technically proficient and practise their art in total solitude then they are going to be pretty lonely most of the time and they are denying themselves the benefits of valuable local advice. Local advice can't be underestimated. You might visit a particular river for a week's holiday over twenty years and think you know it very well but your experience is really only twenty weeks in total and poor in comparison with the person who lives on the river all the time.

Ghillies

The term means a person who attends a sportsman and if you can get the services of a ghillie you should certainly do so. There is not much in the angling literature about ghillies, partly, I suspect, because male anglers think their own efforts less praiseworthy and their contemplation interrupted if they are attended by a ghillie. And so they seem to be disparaging of ghillies generally. If you believed everything you read on this topic you could be forgiven for thinking that ghillies were either dour and silent Scots who cast nothing but disapproving looks at your feeble efforts or lazy drunks who sit about eating your lunch. Naturally this stereotype will cause you some trepidation if you have booked a beat with a ghillie.

John Ashley Cooper is a lone voice in praise of ghillies. He even advises Tweed anglers not to overstrain their boatmen on windy days, when they have a tendency to work too hard in their eagerness to put you into a fish. I must say that I agree with him. I have never experienced anything but unstinting help and advice from ghillies as well as a good deal of courtesy, wit and humour. I find them knowledgable and willing to share this knowledge and tolerant of my more useless efforts. They certainly all try very hard - anyone who doubts this should remember that they have their own reputations to keep up as experts in the locality. I will admit that some of my tackle has found its way into the ghillie's pocket at times but never so often as tackle has been offered generously to me.

I suppose there might be some drunken ghillies but I

108

suspect that anglers themselves play a part in the ghillies' working habits. Drinking and angling do go very well together and there is temptation for an angler to want to celebrate a good fish with the ghillie. This is fine but you need to remember that you are there for only a week and the amount you drink in that week will probably be more than your usual consumption. From a ghillie's point of view, it must seem like a perpetual party as each week of anglers goes through the celebration (or commiseration) process. So it is anglers who are responsible for getting ghillies drunk. You hire the ghillie for the angling - he is not your tour operator and there is no reason why you should expect him to be your drinking companion each evening. If he has worked hard improving your day then he needs rest in the evening.

Some beats expect you to provide a picnic lunch for the ghillie as well as yourself. It is worth finding out about this before you start and inquiring about any preferences for tea, coffee, or alcohol. A flask of hot soup mostly seems welcome but in Ireland you will need tea bags if your ghillie has a volcano kettle. This is a marvellous contraption which carries water and both boils and brews the tea over a tiny fire of twigs.

Overall, the ghillies I have met have been wise men and I have learnt a lot from them. Not least of which is how to ghillie for guests on my club water. There is a good deal of pleasure and satisfaction in attending to your guest's angling and contributing to her success.

How to behave in a boat

Unless you have a lot of boating experience, it is advisable as a general rule not to move in a boat unless instructed and to do everything very slowly. This is important if you want to avoid finding yourself with one foot on the bank and one in the boat, watching in horror as the gap between boat and bank widens. It also makes good sense to wear boots with a ribbed sole so that you don't slip, and a buoyancy jacket is not only a sensible precaution but it is warm too. It is always colder in a boat than wading.

Tweed boats with their swivel seats for the angler are relatively easy but you sit astride the seat in most boats. The biggest difference between angling from a boat and wading, apart from the ease of casting unimpeded, is that your knees are bent much more in a boat. This causes your trousers to ride up and can be uncomfortable. I prefer breeks to trousers for comfort when angling but made a disastrous mistake when I decided to have a pair made for me after finding most ready to wear models were not designed for the female shape. The tailor asked me if I wanted a 'clean silhouette'. Of course I did! I have done for years. To my discomfort later, I found that this means skin tight. All well and good whilst you stand still in front of the mirror with your stomach held in but of no use at all in a boat. It is best to throw fashion and elegance to the winds and get yourself a pair which are cut high in the waist,

. . . you do not want to impale his ear . . .

roomy around the knees and longer than usual in the leg. Also, avoid wellingtons with straps. You will have enough trouble accidentally putting your foot on loose line in the boat without creating extra snags.

But most important of all is to wait and do as you are told. You should never cast in a boat without being constantly aware of the other occupants. There is not only the danger of getting entangled in someone else's line but watch your boatman as you back cast. He will most likely be ducking each time and you do not really want to impale his ear with a fly hook or knock him senseless with a heavy brass tube.

Acceptable boasting

Unless care is taken, it is all too easy to lose friends through injudicious boasting. Traherne has strong feelings on the matter:

'One day when we met as usual, my friend produced five splendid new fish, one of them over 20 lbs; and I had nothing to show. I could see he had no pity for me, and that he was highly pleased with himself; and although I pretended that I rejoiced with him, I was in reality not at all happy and felt very small. This was bad enough, but when, on our separating to resume our sport after lunch, he said to me, 'well, as you are not getting any sport perhaps you would like to read the newspaper (handing me one), instead of fishing this afternoon.' It was almost more than I could stand. However, I declined with thanks and said nothing more, but hated him for half an hour most cordially, and vowed I would pay him back some day.'

My favourite boast is by an angler who wrote an article entitled 'salmon are still eluding my enticing offerings' and mentioned a lost salmon of 20 pounds. How could he know that it weighed 20 pounds if it was never landed? But the article got better still as he detailed all his other records - the best to my mind being 'Goldfish - 1 lb 2 oz, 1968.' I think I would have kept quiet about that one!

Boasting is a surprisingly delicate business. Brown trout anglers rarely boast at all, I suppose because trout angling is a self-contained art which has more to do with you and the fish than you and other anglers. Sea trout and salmon angling is much more passionate and, I think, fair ground for boasting. The problem is how to do it when the rules dictate that you should wait to be asked how you got on. Most anglers do actually ask but if interest is in short supply and you have had a particularly good day then the best way to do it is to take advantage of an angling party made up of young males.

In angling hotels, these parties can usually be heard at least two rooms away from the bar. They are very loud. Their conversations consist of two main variations on a theme. In the first, they are drinking heartily and early - 'come on, have one on James, he's in the chair, excellent day' (they have caught fish). In the second one, they are drinking heavily, slowly and morosely 'I caught a monster in Iceland/Norway/the Falklands' (they have not caught fish). This latter conversation is more usual.

Whichever mode they happen to be in, you will find it difficult to get to the bar as they will be occupying all the best seats but they do have a tendency to send out stray males to find out how everyone else has got on. When approached, fix your eye distastefully on his grimy attire (young, all male groups rarely change for dinner, fearing that to appear in suits will ruin their image and credibility as Ernest Hemingway types), smile sweetly and say in response to his question 'only the one, I'm afraid.' Then pause and add any of the following: 'didn't quite make twenty pounds, unfortunately;' 'sea lice, of course;' or best of all, simply 'each.' At this point the stray male will have little to say but he will return to the pack and they will eye you wonderingly for the rest of the week. They won't talk to you but that doesn't matter - they are not typical anglers.

You won't need to boast again as the hotel staff will do it for you, especially if catching is a bit thin on the ground. They will be heard saying things like 'but the ladies seem to be doing all right.' If no-one takes any notice of you, you can always keep an angling diary and read it out loud to yourself. But don't tell anyone - angling diaries are either incredibly boring or totally scurrilous.

What if you fall in?

It is best not to do this at all. I was asked in Ireland if my buoyancy jacket worked and I was pleased to be able to reply that I didn't know. So far, I have managed to avoid falling into really deep water but I have gone in from some crumbly banks. The getting dry bit afterwards is extremely difficult and the reason why I always carry a 'falling-in' kit in the car boot.

If you do fall in, however, don't worry about being dragged down by your waders. They fill up and act as a sort of buoyancy aid. The main problem with waders full of water is that it

. . . act as a sort of buoyancy aid.

makes getting up the bank hard work as they are so heavy. The important thing is to let your rod go - it will probably get broken by the impact of your fall anyway. Ideally you should spread your arms and legs widely to prevent your going straight to the bottom of the pool but few people are so quick-witted in the middle of a sudden tumble. The regulation advice about keeping your mouth shut to prevent pints of water pouring down your throat should be possible to follow though.

If you are a poised, calm sort of person, then you can follow the advice of a Victorian angler which was related to me by an angling friend. Here, you go with the fall, retaining a firm hold on your rod and simply drift with the flow of the river. From time to time, feel with your left foot for firm ground. As soon as this occurs, you should bend your knees and assume an upright position. I am assured that you will then find yourself in the correct position to resume casting!

CHAPTER EIGHT

POLLUTION

Disillusionment

For most of my life I have believed in the essential superiority
of things British. I was brought up with a firm conviction that
we had the best education system in the world, a free health
service, a generous welfare state and clean water. Bottled water
was something one drank when one was abroad. I also believed
that Yorkshire County Cricket Club could beat any other
cricket club, especially Surrey. This latter could be explained
as a delusion peculiar to Yorkshire people and is no sort of
excuse at all for not realising what was happening elsewhere.
As I grew older, I became disillusioned about the various
welfare services in this country but I still clung on to the clean
water ideal. After all, the rivers in industrial areas might look
foul and dirty, the price I told myself of our industrial success,
but the rivers in rural areas looked clean. It must be a simple
problem of cleaning up the industrial areas.

As my angling career progressed, I began to realise what a
gross naivety this was. Reality set in during regular visits to the
Torridge in the late seventies. On my first trip in 1975, I was
thrilled to be present when there was huge run of autumn
salmon - so thick that fish actually swam between my legs as
I was wading. Trips to the Torridge became regular events,
both in spring and autumn, and I discounted the gloomy
predictions of long established local anglers about the decline
in stocks; certainly catches were unpredictable but the wild
life was wonderful - primroses and daffodils on the banks,

kingfishers flitting up and down stream, and the occasional, magical glimpse of the otter. It was heaven on earth.

And then there were two dry summers and I began to notice that not only were the migratory fish rather thin on the ground but the kingfishers became a rarity, the hatches of insects became scarce and the river weeds coarse and patchy. Finally, I spent a very sad afternoon on the river bank watching cones of dirty brown foam drifting slowly down the once sparkling runs. I blamed local industry and railed against profit hungry farmers and industrialists who poured their filthy effluent into the once lovely river. Belatedly I joined the Torridge Riparian Owners and Fishermen's Association.

But the same picture was emerging elsewhere. I think we were all horrified when the Camel was accidentally polluted, poisoning not only the fish but also a sizeable proportion of the local population. Full realisation of the enormity of the problem didn't set in though until the events of water privatisation began to reveal the full extent of pollution from agriculture and inadequate sewerage treatment as well as the known villains of the piece - factories and mills. It began to dawn on me that I did not understand the intricacies of water quality and pollution effects, nor my possible role in this, although I began to realise that it is possible to disentangle some of the threads and discover that simply blaming 'them' is not a tenable position for any angler to take.

Who pollutes?

Technical books about water pollution are difficult for the novice to follow but the Atlantic Salmon Trust has published a short, comprehensive booklet on water quality requirements for salmon and trout (Solbe, 1988) which is relatively easy to understand. I have also been able to glean information about pesticide and flame retardant chemicals from my brother who is a water chemist in Canada and from colleagues working in a similar area of research in Huddersfield. It seems that there are three main categories of pollution: the obvious one where chemicals and metals are dumped by industry and over which we feel we have little control if the NRA fails to prosecute; the less obvious effects of farming and sewage which are becoming increasingly reported in the press; and individuals' thoughtlessness which causes pollution due to our home and leisure habits - over which we have more direct control.

The first category is usually gross and we expect the water authorities to deal with it. However, it is a sad irony that water authorities only operate from Monday to Friday each week and mostly work on a basis of co-operation and persuasion, trying to encourage firms to be more responsible about effluent discharges. This does nothing to detect the firms who simply wait until the weekend to make loathsome discharges. Even hot water discharges of completely clean water are hazardous to water quality as unnaturally luxuriant weed growth results from them. And we tend not to think how a well- informed workforce could actually impact on employers. If all workers were anglers many more firms would be reported for illegal effluent and a climate would emerge in which employers hesitated to take the easiest and cheapest route for noxious discharges.

The second category of polluters is becoming increasingly understood as we realise that although rivers might be natural drains they cannot cope with the vast amounts of organic matter secreted by farms and sewage plants any more than they can accommodate the inorganic compounds in pesticides and such like. Simply banning the use of pesticides provides less than the answer although these are fairly readily detectable by water authority sampling and analysis. Neither is going 'green,' a return to organic farming, the answer as we make too much organic waste with improved farming techniques and the amount is steadily increasing. Farm wastes (not really wastes because of their good fertilizer value) can be devastatingly polluting. For example, just one litre of silage liquor would completely remove all the oxygen from 9,000 litres of clean, well-aerated water at 15°C - a dilution hardly ever available in ordinary streams. Similarly, slurry not only stinks and pollutes the air after it has been thickly spread on fields but it, too, pollutes water. It is not quite as devastating in its effects as silage liquor but the effects are as harmful overall as there is more of it making its way into rivers.

And there is the problem of excess manure as livestock numbers increase. The Dutch have begun to dry their manure and sell it to third world countries but surely we should think more seriously about the realistic number of animals that our land and its rivers can support. The urge to increase production, to be more efficient with the use of fertilisers, particularly phosphates and nitrates, seriously overloads rivers and changes their characters completely.

Forestry, too, is problematic for river quality. It is not just a problem of acid rain, as there are problems caused by the ploughing and drainage involved in tree plantation which causes the water to run off the land more quickly and silt up the rivers. Also, the trees can cause too much shading of the river so that water temperatures drop too low to sustain natural river life. And when the trees are felled, erosion occurs doing further damage to rivers.

However, we cannot simply blame farmers for accepting short-cuts to production or thoughtlessly allowing sheep dip to run into rivers at times of low water. Domestic waste, particularly sewage, is a major factor in river pollution. Domestic waste is supposedly cleaned up via grit removal, repeated sedimentation processes and biological oxidation to produce clear liquid effluent and a digested sludge.

This sludge can be used in agricultural production if it does not contain too much industrial waste but there is simply too much of it. For example, in my home town, an expensive plant is to be built to burn the sludge. And the 'clean' liquid contains ammonia, nitrite and nitrate, degradable organisms, suspended solids, and resistant organics. This liquid should not constitute a problem as it is weaker than slurry and should be further diluted by the receiving river with the resistant pollution absorbed. However, many sewage works are inefficient. Smith (1989) maintains that they need to be 95% efficient to avoid polluting rivers but many are so overloaded and broken down that they do not achieve even 85% efficiency. Even when repaired, there remain problems with combined systems where storm water goes into sewers. At times of heavy rain and overload, much raw sewage is flushed straight into rivers.

The rivers could probably cope with this if we left the natural flow untouched. But, like salmonoid fish, we humans need clean, well oxygenated water too and we take it away from the rivers into reservoirs and frequently neglect to return it. Under the somewhat euphemistic term 'water abstraction', we take water from high up in the river system where it is particularly clean, use it and then return it, treated, lower down the river. Not only is it not always very clean when it is returned but it is not always returned to the same river. For example, water is taken from Mid Wales for use in Birmingham and returned to a tributary of the Trent as treated sewage.

In global terms, neither trout nor trout anglers lose out as the construction of reservoirs has greatly added to trout habitats and provides inexpensive angling opportunities. But the rivers are losing out. Their natural flow is reduced - and further affected by modern farming methods of drainage which cause the water to flow more quickly off the land. This means that few rivers maintain consistent heights in summer months, affecting both fish and the capacity of the river to minimise pollution via natural dilution. And the habit of offloading treated water into the lower, slower running reaches of rivers affects migrant fish particularly. Although some estuaries such as the Thames and the Tyne are being cleaned up, smaller salmon and sea trout estuaries are becoming increasingly polluted. Migrant fish are very sensitive to water quality and simply will not run through dirty estuaries.

These major causes of pollution may seem far outside the influence of each of us as individuals but we also play our part in the pollution process by the very way we conduct our lives.

For domestic convenience, we add gravely to waste disposal services. For example, for easy gardening we use dangerous pesticides and for efficient cleaning we use harsh and dangerous chemicals. When we are travelling, we pollute the atmosphere and rivers with petrol fumes. Even on trains we cause a long stream of raw sewage. Have you ever thought what happens to sewage when the train is not at a station?

And we carelessly pollute rivers in our pursuit of an enjoyable leisure time. Most water sports are harmful to water quality, mainly via turbulence which causes silting. We stir up sediments and uproot vegetation. Even canoeing causes damage in small streams. Anglers are guilty of pollution and damage too, leaving lengths of nylon on river banks, depositing lead weights in the water and trampling down vegetation.

So we cannot say that polluters are people different from us. Large firms may decide it is cheaper and easier to dump chemicals into the water rather than make them safe and farmers may adopt practices which are aimed at short term profit without thought for the long term effects on the land. Governments, too, may be responsible for polluting the oceans with nuclear waste. But is it 'their' responsibility alone? I don't believe that we, anglers and public alike, are such hopeless dupes, exploited by thoughtless, profit-hungry polluters. These large corporations, governments and farms, big and small, only reflect the overall trend in our habits and preferences. They only 'get away with' large scale pollution because it reflects the small scale, careless pollution in which we all thoughtlessly indulge. We, individually, are convenience minded, meat hungry and careless about our waste.

Perhaps the modern growth of fish farming best illustrates our tacit support for environmentally harmful practice and our dogged refusal to acknowledge our own greed and needs. Whilst the main contaminants in fish farming arise from the food fed to fish and waste products - mainly suspended solids, ammonia, nitrogen and phosphorus - there is little treatment of these wastes despite the existence of suitable technology.

We simply want plentiful and cheap supplies of salmonoid fish for the table and we don't question how they are produced.

In making such fish cheaply available for the average household, we ignore the side effects of factory farming. Just as we have salmonella and mad cow disease because of over-optimistic use of factory farm products and now are aware of the need for constant vigilance about the rapid spread of disease in large flocks and herds, so, too, antibiotics which are extensively used to treat farmed fish need attention. Although much of the antibiotic is lost in the water, many fish bacteria become antibiotic resistant, threatening natural fishes' immune systems. Infection by parasites is also a problem as is the possible escape of farmed fish to rivers taking their farm diseases with them.

Norway, which has farmed salmon for many years, has experienced entire stocks of salmon wiped out in thirty rivers due to the parasite *gyrodactylus salarus*. More recent fish farming activities in Scotland have failed to learn from the Norwegian experience and the situation has become so serious that the North Atlantic Salmon Conservation Organisation (NASCO) believes that stocks of wild salmon are under dire threat of extinction. Farmed salmon escape in large numbers, not only introducing diseases and parasites, but threatening the structure of the gene pool through interbreeding. Farmed salmon may threaten the integrity of entire 'races' of wild fish. Already, one in five of returning salmon netted in Norwegian waters is a farmed fish and the situation may be worse in some parts of Scotland where thousands of farmed salmon escape during gales.

Escapees run up the nearest river and it is not possible in Scotland to resite fish farms away from salmon rivers. Sea trout are also affected, as farmed salmon destroy their spawning redds. Nearly every river in the Highlands contains escaped salmon and there is no evidence that these hybrids will retain their natural instinct to return to the river of their birth although there is one small study being conducted in Scot-

. . . thousands of farmed salmon escape . . .

land. When 200,000 growing salmon were 'liberated' from rafts of cages on Loch Eriboll in Scotland, several were caught on the river Polla (the largest river entering the loch). Fish have since been radio tagged and their behaviour and movements monitored but many more of these studies need to be done and certainly farms need to make the fish cages stronger to prevent escapes.

Does it matter, you probably ask? So, OK, some relatively wealthy and fortunate people may not be able to go off salmon angling but what has this to do with the ordinary person? We need a ready supply of cheap meat, available to all classes of people, so what if we don't see chickens pecking in farmyards, pigs rooting in fields and fish swimming in rivers? Intensive farming may not be pretty but can we afford these old fashioned, expensive and romantic methods; are they just a snobbery on the part of the 'haves' with no thought for the 'have nots' and 'little nots'?

I would argue that it matters very much indeed, on the grounds that intensively farmed food directly causes excessive waste and poses health problems as well as indirectly polluting rivers. Also I think it is morally wrong always to eat meat which is wrapped in polythene, neatly jointed and presented in supermarkets seemingly unsullied by the killing process. My Canadian niece was horrified when she went into a butcher's shop in this country as she had never seen a whole side of meat before. A colleague who was horrified by the fish's struggle on the only occasion she went angling thinks I am inhuman to indulge my passion but she eats both fish and meat. She simply doesn't want to think how it got into the shop. It can't be good for us to be so far removed from the consequences of our actions. If we eat flesh we should at least be aware of what we are doing. If we are aware, we surely would not kill gratuitously nor practise such environmentally harmful, unsavoury and unpleasant methods of meat production.

And fish do matter. Particularly salmonoid fish. They are not just play things for an élite few anglers. They are the single most important indicators of equilibrium in our environment, not for nothing have they been likened to the miner's canary. Exactly like us, they need a good volume of clean water so that they can breathe, eat and have harmful substances diluted and washed away. Unlike us, they are more easily suspectable to pollution. Their sensitivity means that they rapidly decline and disappear where there is pollution. They disappear because we are messing up their environment. What we should be aware of is, if they go, then so will we. We might go more slowly but as we need the same basic quality of water, go we surely will unless we clean up our own water. We should glory in fish because they are proof that we too can live.

How serious is it?
This may all sound a bit heavy. After all, there are countless reservoirs which are sparklingly clear and full of stocked fish and many filthy rivers have been cleaned up. All in all, British

rivers are probably cleaner now than they were 15-20 years ago and now that water privatisation has drawn our attention to the problems of inadequate sewage plants and farm discharges are to be regarded as trade effluents, surely things will get steadily better? We are all green now so the worst must be over? Actually it isn't. Simply ceasing our bad habits will not be enough as we will still suffer the complex and long term effects of eutrophication and biomagnification. In the former, the water is eventually choked by too much rich vegetation and in the latter, the minute effects of toxins magnify as they move from small organisms to larger ones in the food chain. Most people think that eutrophication is something that happens mainly in the Baltic and kills seals or affects this country only in hot weather, closing a few reservoirs - a temporary nuisance much the same as hose pipe bans. And this is partly true. But we do contribute to eutrophication effects all the time by the sheer volume of organic matter we discharge.

The end products of treated sewage might seem harmless but the high concentration of nutrients leads to overabundant algae growth which chokes the water. When the algae dies, its decay in the water adds to the de-oxygenating problem. Basically, with water abstraction at its present level, we cannot afford to discharge more organic waste into the rivers. To be blunt, if we take large quantities of water for domestic use then there won't be enough to flush away our excrement.

Biomagnification of inorganic compounds is less a problem of volume and more one of how non-biodegradable substances maintain a complex balance in the environment. One example of this process is illustrated by substances known as organochlorines. These were immensely popular constituents of pesticides and flame retardant products in the thirties and forties in Western countries because they were highly toxic to insect pests, resistant to heat and decay and seemed to have low toxicity to mammals - in other words, us and our main food supply. Unfortunately, not only can we not get rid of them but their effects are magnified over the years.

The effects on the food chain, whereby the toxins magnify as they progress from small organisms to larger ones, is well understood and no-one now doubts that products such as DDT should not be used. What is perhaps less well known is that organochlorines are irretrievably dispersed in the environment. They have washed into streams, lakes and oceans accumulating in sediment, where they have become so easily identifiable and permanent that they are used as stratigraphic markers - almost like fossils, they indicate the age of the sediment only too well. And they persist in the bodies of small forage organisms. Here they have a habit of working their way backwards and forwards. When residue levels in the water are low, the heavily loaded sediments release toxins back into the environment where they are taken up by small forage organisms and fish.

For example, in the river Colne, dieldrin (an organochlorine insecticide used in the mothproofing of textiles and timber) has been taken up by a small freshwater bivalve, a common filter feeder. This tiny mollusc releases dieldrin back into the water at certain levels. Therefore restocking the river with trout would be of no benefit whatsoever as the basic problem remains. Similarly in North America, a product called Mirex has leaked from industrial wastes around Niagara and is spread by migratory fish. When the fish die after spawning in the headreaches of the river, their carcasses are fed upon by crayfish and snails which pick up the Mirex and pass it on to the native trout (Fox, 1989).

Organochlorines tend to accumulate in fatty tissues and eels are ideal repositories with their high fat content and bottom scrounging nature. And eels move about the world quite a lot! What this means is that we cannot get rid of organochlorines until the sediment containing them is well and truly buried. Western countries have supposedly stopped using organochlorines but we know that they are still extensively used in Eastern Europe and many Third World countries. They not only travel in food chains via water but are also transmitted by air; they are subject to the processes of biomagnification, and they are an international problem. It is no use pointing a finger at governments, it is our problem.

What can we do about it?

The situation might be desperate but it is far from hopeless. The Tweed is a lovely example of a clean river which, as it supports a good stock of salmonoid fish, also supports a good stock of people. The Tweed area never was free from industrial and farming demands and there have had to be compromises between the protection of water quality and availability of finance. What happens on the Tweed is good co-operation between all interested parties. Currie (1989) maintains that 'success in pollution control will depend on an increasingly informed and active public opinion and debate.'

Similarly, the Torridge may have lapsed into a poor state but as soon as anglers, owners, holiday makers, farmers, industrialists and local authorities began talking together and devising plans, matters improved rapidly. The decline of the Torridge has not only been arrested but reversed and now migratory fish are beginning to run the river in greater numbers (not that this means that anglers are being allowed to catch as many as they like). The river still has a long way to go before it will once again be recognisable as the home of Tarka the otter, but steady progress is being made. When people care, when people get more information, they can then act more responsibly. If you involve people in their own river, you soon find out that there are not such clear cut distinctions between polluters and non-polluters, between thoughtfulness and thoughtlessness.

We don't need to feel helpless about gross pollution either although we can only contribute individually. However, in doing so we can form a groundswell of opinion which will act against the complacency which breeds gross pollution. In the first place, if you notice obvious pollution - fish lying dead on the water surface etc - then ring up your local branch of the National Rivers Authority and ask them to investigate. You can take a sample for them but it is important to remember that a small bottleful won't go very far in analysis and it would help if you could give a hint as to what the analysts should be looking for. Water analysis offices are hard pressed so don't expect a full chemical analysis at a moment's notice.

Also willing to help out with instances of obvious pollution are the Salmon and Trout Associations who often have a local Water Resource Office and the Anglers Co-operative Association - a tiny association who have successfully taken out many private prosecutions. You can be a life member or a yearly member for a very reasonable amount. Their address is 23 Castlegate, Grantham, Lincs, NG31 6SW. Also, if you regularly enjoy one particular river, it shouldn't be too much to ask you to join that river's local protection scheme. This will probably cost you less than £10 and such schemes depend upon payments made by non-participating members as much as they do on local efforts.

I think personal behaviour is important too. This means showing respect for the river by careful wading, removing litter, cutting up discarded nylon into tiny pieces etc. Also, there is a lot I think I can do in altering my own lifestyle. In order to transform myself into a non-polluter, I have stopped spraying my roses with pesticides and, to my delight, I find that the greenfly dislike washing up water much more than they ever did the commercial products I used to use. Harsh cleaning products are out and I am using less water. Sharing bath water is fun but going back to a bucket when cleaning the car seemed hard work at first. Not using a hose pipe was something I found quite difficult but it is easier now that I have saved an old dustbin for use as a water butt. I don't wait for droughts but apply my own restrictions all the time. Perhaps we might have less droughts if we were all more thoughtful about water supplies?

Also, I am not going to wait for my local authority to build a new incinerator. I shall try to make less waste. Women have real power in this area because they are most likely to do the shopping and organise household life and can simply opt not to buy products which are over-wrapped or downright dangerous to the environment. Moves to buy goods but return the wrappers to shops can highlight this problem and register a protest as well as ease the perennial problem of overflowing dustbins. Pollution control can, and perhaps should, start in the home. There are many more ways in which each person can become more pollution-conscious but I do not attempt to provide an exhaustive list. It is the initial intention which is the most important step to take.

POSTSCRIPT

Currently women make up only nine percent of all anglers. They all do it companionably; usually with a male partner, but a significant number of women go angling together. Why not add to their numbers? It is a passion rather than an obsession and one that is well worth trying.

Tight lines and loose clothing.

THE END!

GLOSSARY

Breeks; breeches: comfortable trousers which fit snugly below the knee by means of elastic or velcro fasteners.

Bait: anything, other than an artificial fly, placed on a hook with the intention of enticing a fish. Baits fall into two main groups: natural ones such as sprats, worms, shrimps, prawns, and artificial ones made of metal, often referred to as spinners.

Bail arm: a piece of metal at the front of a spinning reel which prevents the nylon line from running off the reel. It can be flicked on or off as needs be but, like most angling tackle, is difficult to explain in a book but easy to understand once you have the object in your hand.

Cast (verb): using the rod to cast the line; to throw it out onto the water in a smooth up, backwards and then forwards movement. There are a number of special casts for difficult conditions such as having no room to make a back cast because of trees and high banks.

Roll Casting: lifting a cast line off the water and rolling it back out again without letting the line go behind you. Best learnt by watching someone demonstrate the action.

Spey Casting: a more complicated method of roll casting where the line is lifted off the water in front of the angler who uses the rod to make a loop with the line so that it can be cast forward without any line going behind the angler. Can be done in single or double movements. Looks impressively fancy and is best taught by an expert in total privacy as most people feel pretty silly when they see their first attempts.

Cast (noun): a length of fine nylon which ties the fly onto the line, sometimes called a leader. They can be bought ready made at tackle shops or you can make your own with a spool of nylon and someone to show you how. Do not try to follow complicated diagrams in books unless you have a lot of technical expertise and endless patience.

Fine Off: an angler's term for the condition of the water in a river when the level is falling and clearing after a flood. A good time to be angling if the water is not dirty.

Fly: supposedly a representation of a natural insect which is tied to the line but can be any creation of feather, fur, tinsel or wool which a fly tier fancies. Can be minute or several inches long. Whole magazines are devoted to fly tying with detailed patterns, rather like knitting magazines.

Ghillie: the person you hire to help you enjoy angling in an area where you will need assistance, such as a boat. Always listen to what your ghillie has to say in the way of advice and you will catch fish; he knows more than any angling author.

Head and Tailing: the movement a salmon makes when it is travelling and not just plopping about. The head shows first and then the tail flicks up slightly. A most exciting sight to anglers as travelling salmon are likely to take your fly. They are more likely to carry on travelling 'though.

Knots: what you use to tie your casts and attach your fly and cast to the main line. Books are full of complicated diagrams of different knots. Best to learn by demonstration but you can always tie a simple thumb knot if stuck. These are supposed not to be strong enough but many people use them without losing too many fish.

Redd: the gravelly bits of river where salmon and sea trout choose to dig out small depressions with their tails and then lay their eggs in them. Disturbing these gravelly bits of river upsets the whole spawning process.

Shrimping: the same as prawning but using the smaller shrimp.

Shrimps are even more difficult to thread onto a needle and attach a hook to without the whole thing dropping to pieces or the needle going into your finger. A method of angling which is largely disapproved of and is banned on many rivers.

Spinner (artificial): any piece of metal which wobbles or spins on the end of the line as it is pulled through the water. Supposed to look like a small fish in distress but looks as much like a long, dangly earring as anything.

Spinner (natural): the last stage of a water borne insect's life. Called a spent spinner as it drops onto the water before dying. Trout love to eat these.

Worming: the use of live, fat worms on a curved needle as a bait for catching salmon.

BIBLIOGRAPHY

Ashley Cooper, John. *The Great Salmon Rivers of Scotland.* Victor Gollancz Ltd, 1980.

Atlantic Salmon Trust, Moulin, Pitlochry, Perthshire, PH16 5JQ.

Berners, Dame Juliana. *A Treatyse of Fysshynge wyth an Angle.* Originally printed by Wynkyn de Worde in The Book of St Albans, 1496. Also, edited by Piscator, privately printed in Edinburgh, 1885.

Cotton, Charles. *The Compleat Angler:* Part Two Appendix see Walton, Isaak, 1676.

Cholmondley-Pennell, H. 'On Hooks, Tackle and Fishing Gear' in *Fishing*, Cholmondley-Pennell, H. The Badminton Library, Longmans, Green & Co, 1889.

Clarkson, J. *Back Casts and Backchat.* Game & Gun Ltd, 1936.

Currie, J C. 'Tweed Water Quality' in *Tweed Towards 2000* ed D Mills, Tweed Foundation, 1989.

Fox, M E. 'Toxins in our fish' *Canadian Sport Fishing.* Fall Issue Vol 7 p25-28, 1989.

Gray, L R N. *Torridge Fishery.* Nicholas Kaye Ltd, 1957.

Falkus, Hugh. *Sea Trout Fishing.* H F & G Witherby Ltd 2nd edition, 1975.

Foster, Muriel. *Days on Sea, Loch and River.* Michael Joseph, 1979.

Francis, Francis. *On Angling.* Longmans, Green & Co, 1867.

Francis, H R. 'Fly Fishing for Trout and Grayling; or 'fine and far off' in *Fishing*, Cholmondley-Pennell, H. The Badminton Library, Longmans, Green & Co, 1889.

Kelson, G M. *The Salmon Fly*. Wyman & Sons, 1895.

Koller, Larry. *The Treasury of Angling*. Paul Hamlyn, 1966.

Nelson, W. *Fishing in Eden*. H, F & G Witherby, 1922.

Paterson, W & Behan, P. *Salmon and Women: the feminine angle*. H, F & G Witherby, 1990.

Pearce, C R. 'Sunshine/Shadow Strategy' in *Trout and Salmon Fishing*. (ed) Eaton, Roy, EMAP National Publications, 1981.

Ritz, Charles. *A Fly Fisher's Life*. Max Reinhardt, 1959.

Solbe, J. *Water Quality for Salmon and Trout*. The Atlantic Salmon Trust, 1988.

Smith, P. 'Water - a time for change' *Salmon, Trout and Sea Trout*, Sept p58-59, 1989.

Thelwell, N. *A Plank Bridge by a Pool*. Methuen, 1978.

Traherne, Major J P. 'Salmon Fishing with a Fly' in *Fishing*, Cholmondley-Pennell, H. The Badminton Library, Longmans, Green & Co, 1889.

Venables, Bernard. *The Angler's Companion*. George Allen & Unwin Ltd, 1959.

Waddington, R. *Catching Salmon*. David and Charles, 1978.

Walker, Richard. *No Need to Lie*. E M Art & Publishing Ltd in conjunction with George Allen and Unwin, 1964.

Walton, Isaak. *The Compleat Angler*, reproduced in facsimile from the first edition, 1653, and published by A & C Black Ltd 35 Bedford Row, London.

Wiggan, Maurice. *Fly Fishing*. English Universities Press Ltd, 1958.

Willcock, Colin (ed). *The Penguin Guide to Fishing*. Penguin Books, 1964.